The Knights Templar

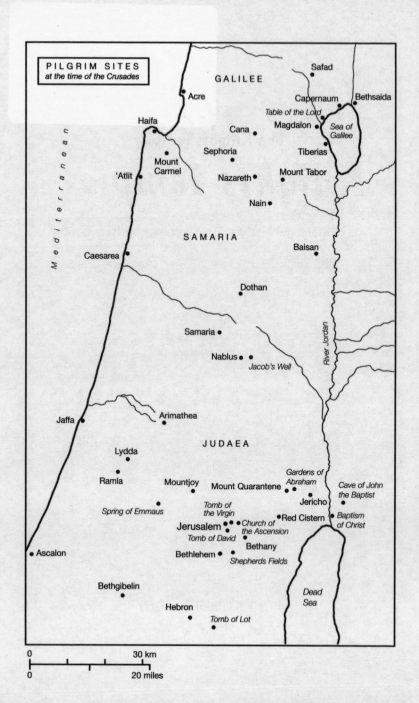

PILGRIM SITES
at the time of the Crusades

GALILEE

Acre

Haifa

Cana

Sephoria

Mount
Carmel

Nazareth

Nain

'Atlit

Mediterranean

SAMARIA

Caesarea

Safad

Capernaum

Bethsaida

Table of the Lord

Magdalon

*Sea of
Galilee*

Tiberias

Mount Tabor

Baisan

Dothan

Samaria

Nablus

Jacob's Well

River Jordan

Jaffa

Arimathea

JUDAEA

Lydda

Ramla

Mountjoy

Mount Quarantene

Spring of Emmaus

*Tomb of
the Virgin*

Jerusalem

Tomb of David

Bethlehem

Ascalon

Bethgibelin

Hebron

Tomb of Lot

*Gardens of
Abraham*

*Cave of John
the Baptist*

Jericho

Red Cistern

*Baptism
of Christ*

*Church of
the Ascension*

Bethany

Shepherds Fields

*Dead
Sea*

| 0 | | 30 km |
| 0 | | 20 miles |

The
Knights Templar

The History and Myths of the Legendary Military Order

SEAN MARTIN

POCKET ESSENTIALS

This edition published in 2014
by Pocket Essentials
PO Box 394, Harpenden, Herts, AL5 1JX, UK

A CIP catalogue record for this book is available from the British Library.

ISBN
978-1-84243-563-2 (print)
978-1-84243-565-6 (epub)
978-1-84243-566-3 (kindle)
978-1-84243-567-0 (pdf)

17, 18, 20, 19, 16

Typography by Avocet Typeset, Somerton, Somerset

Printed and bound in Great Britain by Clays Ltd, St Ives plc

'What is history, but a fable agreed upon?'

Napoleon Bonaparte

Acknowledgements

Thanks are due to Nicholas Mark Harding, for lending me certain not-so-ancient tomes on this occasion, Mike Paine for the usual moral support, and Richard Leigh, for his advice relating to matters discussed in Chapter 4.

A Note on the Revised Paperback Edition

For this new paperback edition, I have revised the Afterword, adding new material relating to the Templars' connection to the Turin Shroud. The Bibliography and Endnotes have been expanded, and several errors lingering from earlier editions laid to rest.

Contents

Introduction:
The Temple and the Myth

On the morning of 21 January 1793, the French king, Louis XVI, was led out into the Place de la Concord in Paris to face execution. He stepped up onto the platform where the guillotine had been erected, and turned to address the huge crowd who had come to watch him die. He announced that he forgave the revolutionary council who had voted for his death, and then gave himself over to the executioner. The blade fell at 10:15. The executioner held Louis' decapitated head up by the hair to show that the king was dead. What happened next, according to some sources,[1] took the crowd by surprise: a man jumped up onto the platform and dipped his fingers in the dead king's blood. He held his hand aloft and shouted 'Jacques de Molay, thus you are avenged!' The crowd cheered, understanding the reference to the last Templar Grand Master, who was burned as a relapsed heretic in 1314; the long-held popular rumour that one day the Templars would have their revenge on the French monarchy – which had brought the Order down on dubious charges of heresy, blasphemy and sodomy – seemed to have come true. Indeed, speculation was rife that the Templars were among the instigators of the revolution that had swept through France in 1789, ultimately claiming the lives of Louis and his queen, Marie Antoinette.

Modern historians would scoff at such a notion, but it certainly illustrates the unique hold the Knights Templar have had on the European imagination ever since they emerged from obscurity in the late 1120s. They have been seen as heroic soldier-monks guarding pilgrims to the Holy Land during the Crusades, defenders of Holy Church who fought alongside Richard the Lionheart. Their critics – in their own time, usually annalists and commentators from rival monastic orders – accused them of the sins of pride and arrogance, and were deeply suspicious of the air of secrecy that hung over the Order like a veil. To Walter Scott, they were evil, and he made them the villains of *Ivanhoe*. Modern historians have tried to show that the Templars were a highly efficient military organisation made up largely of illiterates who were in reality very ordinary; their achievements were to be the creation of the first standing army in Europe since the days of the Roman Empire, and – as the first bankers in the West – the mediaeval organisation that did most to pave the way for modern capitalism.

Those of a more speculative cast of mind – and there have been many over the centuries – have seen the Order variously as an esoteric brotherhood, hungry for forbidden knowledge; apostates involved in diabolic practices who were the witches' next of kin; a mysterious political entity that has guided world affairs since their suppression, clandestinely directing events from behind the scenes; and renegade Christians who supported and sheltered heretics, forged links with occult groups in the Arab world and who discovered the Turin Shroud, the Ark of the Covenant and the Holy Grail.

Books about the Templars tend to fall into two camps: what could be termed orthodox and speculative. The former camp is represented by academics such as Malcolm Barber, whose studies *The New Knighthood* and *The Trial of the Templars* are critically acclaimed and are the books one should consult if one is seeking a comprehensive treatment of Templar history. The latter camp of speculative writers has spawned a thriving industry of books containing a multitude of theories ranging from the plausible to the risible. In France – where there is a vast literature on the Templars – the Order holds a position similar to that of Glastonbury in England, a sort of historical *tabula rasa* onto which almost anything can be projected.

This book will trace the Templar story, from its beginnings in the early twelfth century, through to the suppression of the Order by the Pope in 1312 and the execution of Jacques de Molay two years later. The myths surrounding them will be examined in a later chapter. Whether or not there is any truth to them is, of course, another matter.

The Rise of the Order
of the Temple
(1119–45)

The Order of Poor Knights of Christ and the Temple of
Solomon, more commonly known as the Order of the Temple or
the Knights Templar, was founded by the French nobleman
Hugues de Payen in around the year 1119 in Jerusalem. The Holy
City, back in Christian hands ever since the First Crusade twenty
years previously, was the main destination for pilgrims from
Europe. They came in their droves, unaware of the dangers that
lay ahead – the roads around Jerusalem were notorious for the
bands of robbers that haunted them, preying on the travellers to
the Holy Places. Sometimes these robbers were Saracens; sometimes they were lapsed crusaders. To counter this threat, Hugues
de Payen gathered a group of nine knights together to protect
the pilgrims.

Hugues and his brothers did not look like the knights of
popular imagination. They had no money, wore clothes that were
donated to them and suffered from a constant shortage of new
recruits and equipment in the early years of their existence. Yet
by 1129, at the Council of Troyes, the Templars had become
almost overnight the heroes of Christian Europe, and between
1139 and 1145, the Pope issued a series of three papal bulls that
gave the Templars almost total power, making them answerable
to none save the pontiff himself. It was one of the most remarkable turnarounds of the Middle Ages, if not of all European
history.

If we are to understand why and how the Templars rose to such prominence so quickly after such apparently humble beginnings, we need to take a look at the background to the Jerusalem in which they found themselves at their inception, and trace the history of the city itself, right back to the original Temple of Solomon.

The First Temple

The original temple in Jerusalem was the Temple of Solomon, built by the great king around the year 950 BC. The site – known ever since as the Temple Mount or the Temple platform – had been chosen by his father, King David, who recognised it as the spot on which Abraham had prepared his son Isaac for sacrifice.

Abraham is thought to have lived 18 centuries before Christ, and was one of the founding fathers of the Jewish nation. His attempt to sacrifice Isaac symbolised both his obedience to God and his fear of Him. As Abraham raised the knife to kill his child, God spoke and ordered him to stay his hand; Abraham complied, and God was pleased. He promised Abraham that He would 'shower blessings' on him and make his people, the Jews, 'as many as the stars of heaven and the grains of sand on the seashore'.[2] The spot of the attempted sacrifice came to represent, for the Jews, their unbreakable bond with God.

Solomon constructed his Temple as a dwelling place for the name of God, which resided in the Holiest of Holies with the Ark of the Covenant, guarded by two giant golden cherubim. The Ark contained the stone tablets on which were written the Ten Commandments that Moses brought down from Mount Sinai. Like the story of Abraham and Isaac, the Commandments were tangible proof of the Jews' covenant with the Almighty.

Solomon was reputedly the wisest of men, and his reign

marks a high point of the Jewish nation; the Temple that he constructed in Jerusalem was said to have profound wisdom embodied in its architecture, and was a place of awe, pilgrimage and devotion. Its treasure – altars, basins, snuffers, ladles, fire pans, candelabra, all made from gold or bronze – was legendary. The Temple itself was to become the stuff of fable, 'a house of prayer for all nations' (Isaiah 56.7) that was to have a profound influence on the imaginations of succeeding generations, a symbol of God's presence on Earth.

But the high-water mark of Solomon's reign did not last. Israel was occupied by successive invasions from the East, first by the Assyrians, and then, in 586 BC, by the Chaldeans. Their king, Nebuchadnezzar, ordered that the Temple be destroyed and the Jewish people taken into slavery at Babylon. The Chaldeans were, in turn, ousted by the Persians, whose king, Cyrus, allowed the Jews to return home in 515 BC and rebuild the temple.

Political uncertainty in the second century BC led Israel to appeal for protection from Rome. What initially started as diplomatic intervention became, by the time of Julius Caesar's visit in 47 BC, occupation. This in turn led to much dissent and the formation of groups opposed to Roman rule. There was a general expectation of a Messiah, who would arrive and liberate the Jewish people once and for all from the tyranny of occupation. Some believed this to be Jesus, whose followers were outlawed and persecuted, being seen as agitators and, in some cases, terrorists. In 66 AD, the Jews revolted. The Romans retaliated brutally, crushing the uprising; the Temple was destroyed for a second time. In 134, there was another uprising, led by Simeon ben-Koseba, who, according to the Rabbi Akiba, really was the long-awaited Messiah. This was also crushed, leading to the Jews being banned from entering Jerusalem at all.

By the early fourth century, Jerusalem was becoming a Holy City for a second faith, that of the new religion of Christianity. In 312, the Roman Emperor Constantine converted, and he ordered that churches be built over the site of Christ's birth in Bethlehem, and those of his Crucifixion and Resurrection in Jerusalem; the latter church became known as the Church of the Holy Sepulchre. However, Constantine's nephew and successor, Julian the Apostate, did not share his uncle's beliefs, and the Empire returned to paganism. In a blatant attempt to antagonise Christians, Julian began to rebuild the Temple (not that he had any time for the Jews, who were persecuted with equal zeal). The project did not progress smoothly, and was abandoned upon Julian's death in 363. Jerusalem seemed destined never to have another Temple.

The Temple and the Mosque

With its administration creaking, the Roman Empire divided into two in the fourth century. The western half would still be ruled from Milan (Rome having lost its capital status in 286), while the eastern half had Byzantium – now renamed Constantinople – as its capital. The Byzantines built a new church (or possibly a monastery) on the Temple mount, but were driven briefly out of Jerusalem by the Sassanids in 610. For the first time in centuries, the Temple platform passed back to the Jews, and work started on rebuilding the Temple. It was never finished: Christians regained control, tore down the building, and the Temple Mount became a rubbish tip.

In 638, Jerusalem surrendered to the Caliph Omar, and the city fell into Muslim hands. Since its founding by the Prophet Muhammad with the *hijrah* of 622 – when the Prophet migrated from Mecca to Medina, thus beginning the Muslim calendar –

Islam had spread rapidly throughout the Middle East. The Byzantines seemed powerless to stop its progress, and retreated north. Jerusalem was sacred to Muslims, in particular the Temple Mount area, as it was the site of the Prophet's ascension to heaven. Upon his entry into Jerusalem, Omar had gone there to pray, and resolved to build the al-Aqsa mosque on the site. Towards the end of the seventh century, a second, even more impressive, mosque was built on the Temple Mount, the Dome of the Rock. Jerusalem was further than ever from Christian hands.

The First Crusade

Islam continued to impinge upon Christian Europe, with most of the Mediterranean and the Iberian peninsula falling under Muslim control during the seventh and eighth centuries. By the middle of the eleventh century, a new Islamic threat had emerged, from the Seljuk Turks. Originally from central Asia, they had moved inexorably westwards, conquering Baghdad and converting to Islam in the process. They had Constantinople in their sights, and in 1071 defeated the imperial army at Manzikert in Armenia. Within a decade, they had also taken Nicaea and controlled the whole of Asia Minor. The Byzantine empire was now solely comprised of its lands west of the Bosphorous, and it was to the West that the Byzantine emperor Alexius looked for help to stave off certain annihilation.

In the spring of 1095, a delegation arrived at the Council of Piacenza in northern Italy. Although the eastern and western churches had split decisively in 1054, the Pope, Urban II, had made conciliatory moves towards Constantinople by rescinding Alexius' excommunication, and it was therefore with some hope that the eastern delegation appealed to the council. Its plea for help did not fall on deaf ears. Urban called for a meeting of bishops to address the problem, to be held that November in Clermont.

On Tuesday 27 November 1095, after a week-long ecclesiastical conference in the cathedral, Urban addressed a huge crowd outside the walls of Clermont. He called on those assembled to desist from fighting one another, internecine warfare having dogged Europe ever since the sack of Rome in 410; he called instead that their energies be better spent fighting the infidel in the East, and returning Jerusalem into the arms of Mother Church. The crowd was ecstatic, with cries of '*Deus lo volt*!' – 'God wills it!' – echoing from the city walls. A bishop and a cardinal immediately knelt before Urban and begged to join the campaign. The First Crusade had begun.

After arriving in Constantinople in late 1096, the crusaders marched south, taking Nicaea in June of the following year. Edessa and Antioch both capitulated in 1098, and the crusaders finally arrived outside the walls of the Holy City on 7 June 1099. Jerusalem finally fell on 15 July after a ferocious bloodbath. It was the first time it had been in Christian hands for 461 years. One of the Crusade's leaders, Godfroi de Bouillon – after refusing to be called king on the grounds that only Christ had the right to that title – was proclaimed Defender of the Holy Sepulchre, and the Latin Kingdom of Jerusalem was thus established. In Europe, it became known as Outremer – the land beyond the sea.

The New Knighthood

After the victory of the First Crusade, most of the surviving crusaders returned to Europe, leaving Baldwin de Boulogne – Godfroi having died unexpectedly in July of 1100 – to assume the title of the first King of Jerusalem. His domain stretched south to the Red Sea, and north as far as Beirut. Above that lay the County of Tripoli, ruled by Raymond de Saint-Gilles, Count of Toulouse. North of Tripoli was the Principality of Antioch, whose ruler was Bohemond of Taranto. The two remaining Christian kingdoms were the County of Edessa to the north-east – the first Latin kingdom to be established by the crusaders, in 1098 – and Cilician Armenia to the north-west, in what is now Turkey. Outremer, being as it was a collection of small, largely coastal kingdoms ruled by allied European nobles, was modelled on the feudal system that had dominated Europe since the late Dark Ages.

After the fall of the Roman Empire in the West, Europe was ravaged by successive waves of invaders: the Saracens and Magyars from the east; the Vikings from the north. In addition, kingdoms were constantly engaged in squabbles with one another, and this uncertain political climate gave rise to what became known – from the sixteenth century onwards – as the feudal system. None of the kingdoms of Europe had a centralised power base and, as a result, monarchs were largely powerless to protect their people. In order to secure some form of protection and to feed his family, a man would have to offer his services to the local landowner. With no such thing as a standing army, the landowner would always need to call upon men to fight to protect his dominions. Thus, the man swore loyalty to the lord, and became known as his vassal. Vassalage required that the man swear an oath of loyalty to his lord and be on call to fight for him whenever the need arose. In return, the lord would provide the vassal with land (or sometimes the income from ecclesiastical institutions), which would feed the vassal's family and also bring in revenue to the lord's exchequer from taxes levied on the vassal's land.

It was against this background that knights began to emerge. The lord–vassal system may have had its origins in the old

Roman practice of commendation, in which a soldier would pledge service to an officer of superior rank in return for a reward to be decided by the officer. Usually it took the form of a grant of land, which was known as a benefice. European monarchs, such as Charlemagne, began to adopt this practice, and gave their best warriors grants of land. The warriors in turn would take on vassals to work the land on their behalf, thus leaving them essentially free to develop their military and equestrian skills. However, although both knight and vassal were made to swear oaths of loyalty to their lord, it was possible for them to move on to serve another lord if the protection provided proved to be inadequate, or if the lord in question was deposed or killed. In most cases, though, the relationship between lord, knight and vassal became hereditary.

The crusaders who stormed Jerusalem in the summer of 1099 were a mixture of lords, knights and vassals, and all had been promised full remission of their earthly sins for taking part in the Crusade, or pilgrimage, as it was euphemistically called. The lure of remission also proved an enticing prospect for other, less savoury characters. This latter group included convicted criminals and excommunicates, who used the Crusade as a means of escaping punishment back home. Thus, when the city was safely in Frankish hands, most of the surviving crusaders returned to Europe, having achieved their objectives in taking the Holy City and also having absolved themselves of all wrongdoing. Baldwin then faced the problem of ruling a kingdom with no standing army to protect it.

Despite the fact that all the major cities and ports of Outremer were in Christian hands, the kingdom's roads were anything but secure. Even when under Muslim control, the Holy Land had continued to attract Christian pilgrims, and now that a Christian king sat on the throne of Jerusalem, they came in even greater numbers. The sites they visited were known simply as The Holy Places, and were scattered throughout the Kingdom: Sephoria was where the Virgin had spent her childhood; in Bethlehem, there was the site of the Nativity; the River Jordan was the scene of Christ's baptism by John the Baptist (whose cave dwelling was nearby); while various locales around the Sea of Galilee were witnesses to Christ's ministry. Mount Tabor was the site of the Transfiguration, while the road from Jerusalem to Jericho was the location of the Good Samaritan's charity.

However, the pilgrims were never safe once they were outside the walls of Jerusalem, as attacks by bands of Saracen robbers were frequent. Even as early as 1106, there were reports of trouble. A Russian abbot by the name of Daniel wrote of his visit to the tomb of St George at Lydda that year:

> 'And there are many springs here; travellers rest by the water but with great fear, for it is a deserted place and nearby is the town of Ascalon from which Saracens sally forth and kill travellers on these roads. There is a great fear too, going up from that place into the hills.'[3]

But that was nothing compared to Galilee:

> 'This place is very dreadful and dangerous… many tall palm trees stand about the town like a dense forest. This place is terrible and difficult of access for here live fierce pagan Saracens who attack travellers at the fords.'[4]

Thirteen years later, things had got even worse. At Easter 1119, a group of 700 pilgrims was attacked by Saracens on the road to the River Jordan; 300 were killed and 60 carried off into slavery. Later that year, the forces of Roger, Bohemond II of Antioch's regent, were ambushed and killed at the Field of Blood. This led to a flurry of requests for further aid from the West, and a council of Church leaders met in Nablus in January 1120 to address the issue.

At the time that Roger and his men met their fate on the Field of Blood, Baldwin's successor, Baldwin II, had been on the throne of Jerusalem for a year. It is thought that at some point during 1119 he granted an audience to two French noblemen, Hugues de Payen from Champagne and Godfrey de St Omer from Picardy. Together with seven other knights, they proposed to guard the pilgrims as they made their way to and from the Holy Places. But they would not do so as regular knights – they would live as a small monastic community, following the rule of St Augustine. Baldwin liked the idea. Manpower had always been an issue in Outremer and the fact that Hugues and his brethren were prepared to live as monks meant that they would be, in theory, more dependable than some of the rabble who had taken part in the First Crusade. The king approved the plan and, on Christmas Day, Hugues and Godfrey swore vows of poverty, chastity and obedience before Baldwin and Warmund of Picquigny, the Patriarch of Jerusalem, in the Church of the Holy Sepulchre, and Baldwin gave them quarters at the al-Aqsa mosque on the Temple platform. The Order of Poor Knights of Christ and the Temple of Solomon, the Order of the Temple, the Knights Templar, was born.

Within weeks of the founding of their order, the Templars were introduced to the clergy at the Council of Nablus. The nine knights were accepted by those present, and Hugues and his brothers began their task of policing the kingdom. The other founding knights were: Payen de Montdidier; André de Montbard; Archambaud de St Aignan; Geoffrey Bisol; two knights known only by their Christian names of Roland and Gondemar; while the ninth member remains unknown.

The Templars' first decade is their least documented. After Nablus, we can only assume that they continued to live as monks in the 'Temple of Solomon' (the crusaders' name for the al-Aqsa mosque) and to protect the pilgrims who would arrive by boat at ports such as Jaffa. Despite their poverty and lack of decent armour and weapons, they began to attract supporters from the West. Fulk V, Count of Anjou, met Hugues de Payen on his pilgrimage to Outremer in 1120, and was so impressed with Hugues and his nascent order that he enrolled as an associate of the Templars, pledging to give them an annual income of 30 *livres angevines*. Inspired by Fulk's example, several other French nobles did the same, perhaps the most important of them being Hugh, Count of Champagne.

Hugh had first visited Outremer in 1104, where he remained for four years. He returned again in 1114. On one of these occasions, he had been accompanied by Hugues de Payen. Hugues was one of his vassals, Payen being downriver from Troyes, where Hugh had his court. (In fact, Hugues may have even been related to his lord.) By the time Hugues and his eight companions took their vows in the Church of the Holy Sepulchre, Hugh had once again returned to France. He returned to the Holy Land for the last time in 1125, when he finally joined the Templars. But the full significance of Hugh's relationship to the Templars would have to wait another four years before becoming apparent.

In 1127, with the Templars still – according to the traditional story – only nine knights strong and struggling to recruit new members, King Baldwin II sent Hugues de Payen and several other Templar brethren on a major diplomatic mission to Europe. That Hugues was chosen for such an important job suggests that, contrary to the stories of the Templars being 'poor knights', they were in fact by this time quite highly regarded in

Outremer. In addition, Hugues took several knights with him, which, if they really were still only nine members strong, would have left only a few brethren back in Outremer. Indeed, chroniclers such as Michael the Syrian (d.1199), who was one of the first to document the Templars, believed that the Order had about 30 serving knights enlisted by the time of Baldwin's embassy.

The Templar delegation sailed to France, probably in the autumn of 1127, with William of Bures, the Prince of Galilee, and Guy of Brisbarre, Lord of Beirut. William and Guy's mission was to persuade Fulk of Anjou to marry Baldwin's daughter, Melisende, and thereby stand to inherit the throne of Jerusalem, as Baldwin had no male heir. Whether Hugues' presence in the delegation was meant to persuade Fulk, who was one of the Templars' earliest supporters and donors, is not known, but even if it were, Hugues had been charged by Baldwin with another mission: to recruit knights for a projected crusade against Damascus, and to get the Templars officially recognised by the western Church.

The mission was a stunning success: Fulk agreed to return to Outremer and marry Melisende; many new recruits for Baldwin's Damascene Crusade were signed up; and, perhaps most importantly of all, Hugues met St Bernard of Clairvaux. It is from then on that, with St Bernard's unwavering support, the Knights Templar emerged from the shadows on to the stage of European history in quite spectacular fashion.

The Council of Troyes

St Bernard of Clairvaux was the most influential churchman of his time. A Burgundian noble, he was born at Fontaines-les-Dijons in 1090. While he was still in his mother's womb, a devout had predicted a great future for Bernard, and he seems to have grown into adulthood with a particular fervour and vision. Apparently a charismatic man of quite violent passions, he sought out a religious order whose austerity might help temper his volatile nature, and he entered the Cistercian order at Cîteaux in 1113 with 30 or so fellow Burgundian nobles. Three years later, he led a small group of monks to found a new Cistercian house in the nearby valley of Wormwood, which they renamed Clairvaux, Valley of Light. Significantly, the land had been given to them by Hugh of Champagne, around the time of the Count's second pilgrimage to Outremer. The new foundation at Clairvaux under Bernard quickly became a magnet for the zealous, and the house flourished.

It is not known exactly when Bernard (he became a saint in 1174, a mere 21 years after his death) first became aware of the Templars or met Hugues de Payen. It is probable that King Baldwin wrote to Bernard in 1126 asking him to help devise a Rule for the Order, and to help win for them both recognition and support in the West. Bernard was aware of the situation in the East, and realised that what Outremer needed were knights ready for active military service, not 'singing and wailing monks'.[5] Bernard's keen appreciation of the situation in the East most probably derived from his friendship with Hugh of Champagne, who had returned to the Holy Land for the third and final time in 1125, when he became a fully fledged Templar, and also from André de Montbard, who was not only one of the original nine knights, but was also Bernard's uncle. If Hugues and the Templar delegation did indeed sail to Europe during the autumn passage of 1127, then it is possible that Bernard met the Templar Grand Master towards the end of that year, or the following spring before Hugues started his mission proper, which would culminate with the Council of Troyes in January 1129.

As soon as Hugues arrived in Europe, things appeared to start moving very quickly. The Templars received their first grant of land in the West, with a house, a grange, a meadow and a tenement in Provins being given to the Order in October 1127, a gift from Hugh of Champagne's successor, Theobald, Count of Blois. Theobald also gave his vassals permission to donate freely to the Order from their own holdings of land. The Count of Flanders, William Clito, also donated to the Order around this time, as did his successor, Thierry of Alsace, after William's death in battle on 27 May 1128. Four days later, Hugues was in Anjou, where he witnessed Fulk take the Cross (a vow to defend Christianity from the infidel). On 17 June, he attended the wedding of Fulk's eldest son, Geoffrey, to Matilda, daughter of Henry I of England, which then left Fulk free to travel to Jerusalem as Baldwin had hoped. Further grants of land and money were made to Hugues, and it seems likely that the wedding led directly to Hugues being invited to England in the summer of 1128. Hugues' visit to England resulted in the establishment of the first Templar house, or preceptory, in London, at the north end of what is now Chancery Lane, in addition to gifts of money from the king and the acquisition of several sites outside of the capital. From England, Hugues travelled to Scotland before spending the autumn in Flanders, receiving further donations and preparing for Troyes.

When Hugues de Payen spoke before the Council of Troyes on 13 January 1129, he did so in front of an august assembly of churchmen. Not only was Bernard there in person (despite the fact that he was suffering from a fever), but also Stephen Harding, Abbott of Cîteaux, the Archbishops of Sens and Rheims, ten bishops, Count Theobald of Champagne and, according to Jean Michel, the council's scribe, 'several others whom it would be tedious to record'. In addition to Hugues, the Templars were represented by Godfrey de St Omer, Geoffrey Bisol, Payen de

Montdidier, Roland and Archambaud de St Aignan.[6] The whole delegation was presided over by the Papal Legate, Matthew of Albano.

In his speech, Hugues described the origins of the Order and the rule by which they lived: attending the offices; communal meals taken in silence; plain clothing; no women. Each brother swore vows of poverty, chastity and obedience upon entering the Order. As the brethren were frequently called out of the Temple on knightly business, they were each allowed one horse (although this was later increased to three), and a handful of servants. When away from the Temple, recitation of paternosters replaced hearing the offices. Knights and servants alike were under Hugues' command, with the whole order being answerable to the Patriarch of Jerusalem.

After some debate, the Council, under Bernard's supervision, drew up what became known as the Latin Rule of the Templars, which was based on the rule described by Hugues in his speech. It consisted of 73 clauses and regulated every aspect of Templar life. In addition to keeping the observances that the Order was already following, the Latin Rule advised the brethren how to admit newcomers to the Order, and how they should be vetted before being sworn in; at what age newcomers could join (boys being advised to wait until they were old enough to bear arms); how long brothers could serve for (which was usually a fixed term before allowing them to return to secular life if they so wished); how to reprimand miscreants and what offences would lead a brother to be expelled from the Order (such as deserting the battlefield, leaving a castle without permission or via an unauthorised exit), and so on. Knights were to wear white habits, to signify chastity and purity, while sergeants and squires were to wear brown or black (it must be remembered that the majority of Templars were not knights, but those who worked in the elaborate support network in the West that allowed them to remain on military duty in the East). Chastity and purity were also symbolised by a linen cord or belt that all Templars wore, regardless of rank. The brethren's clothing and the bridles of their horses were to be unostentatious, avoiding such concessions to fashion as pointed shoes with laces and long hair. The Rule demanded short hair and beards were mandatory.

There were two meals a day, around noon and then again at dusk, which were to be communal and silent, punctuated only by a reading from the scriptures. Meat was to be eaten only three times a week. No one was to get down from table unless there was a disturbance amongst the horses, or there was an impending attack. Physical relations with women were prohibited (although married men were admitted to the Order, provided they had their wives' consent). A yet more serious a crime was homosexuality, which was seen as being as bad as killing a fellow Christian. Idle talk was forbidden, with brethren expected to spend their free time maintaining the horses, equipment and clothing, or spending time in prayer.

Naturally, the churchmen gathered at Troyes had a great deal of clerical experience between them, but very little of campaigning in Outremer, so the Rule was more monastic than military, being principally concerned with the spiritual welfare of the Order's brethren. (It does make a few concessions to the actual physical conditions in the East, by allowing the brothers to wear linen shirts in the summer instead of the more customary European woollen equivalent.) Whatever shortcomings there were in the original 1129 Rule, they would later be rectified in the 1160s, and then again in the 1260s. By the time of the Order's downfall, the Rule had grown to contain 686 clauses.

Daily life in a Templar preceptory was much the same as that of a Western monastery. The day would begin (during the summer months) with matins at 4:00am, which comprised the saying of 13 paternosters. The brothers were then permitted a brief sleep until the division bell summoned them to prime at 6:00am, when the first mass of the day was said. Terce was at 8:00am, and sext at 11:30am, which was followed by the first meal of the day. Usually the knights ate first, followed by the sergeants. Nones was at 2:00pm, followed by vespers at 6:00pm. The evening meal would then be taken, with the final office of the day, compline, being said around 8:00pm. As the winter months brought shorter daylight hours, the offices would be compressed so that matins would always begin after first light, and compline would similarly occur around the onset of twilight.

'A Certain New Monster'

When Hugues de Payen returned to Outremer after the Council of Troyes, he did so as the head of an order which was now in a greatly enhanced position. Nevertheless, the Templars were not universally welcomed by all quarters of the Church. During the tenth and eleventh centuries, the Church had gone through a great wave of reforms championed by Pope Gregory VII (1073–85), which had seen the establishment of such houses as Cluny and Cîteaux. The reformers of Bernard's generation and the generation before stressed spiritual purity untainted by politics and especially bloodshed. They strove to maintain a distance between temporal monarchy and spiritual matters. The English archdeacon and historian Henry of Huntingdon was to describe the mix of monk and soldier as 'a certain new monster', while Guigo, the prior of La Grande Chartreuse, wrote to Hugues to warn of the dangers of mixing the military and the monastic:

'It is useless indeed for us to attack exterior enemies if we do not first conquer those of the interior... Let us first purge our souls of vices, then the lands from the barbarians.'[7]

Guigo implored Hugues to read the letter to all the brethren and even went so far as to send the letter twice via different couriers to ensure that at least one copy reached its destination.

Another letter exists from around this time addressed to Templar brethren, authored by a 'Hugues', although this has never been proven to be Hugues de Payen. The writer has simply signed himself as '*Hugo peccator*' – Hugh the Sinner – and it is conceivable that it is the work of the theologian Hugh of St Victor. Regardless of authorship, the letter is ample evidence that external criticism of the Order had filtered through the ranks. It begins '...we have heard that certain of you have been troubled by persons of little wisdom',[8] and proceeds to warn the brethren of the Devil and all his works. Hugo stresses the need for the brothers to be mindful of their inner state, and to accept their lot, reminding them that their personal salvation has to be worked for.

Whether or not Hugues de Payen wrote the '*Hugo peccator*' letter, he seems at the very least to have been aware of it, as he asked Bernard of Clairvaux no fewer than three times to compose a defence of the Order, as if to settle the matter once and for all. Bernard, by now the Order's most prominent supporter, did not disappoint. The treatise he wrote, *In Praise of the New Knighthood*, draws a distinction between the old, secular knighthood that had predominated since the days of Charlemagne, and the new, monastic knighthood as personified by the Templars. By doing so, Bernard was going against the drift of Gregory VII's reforms, which had been marked by an aversion to all forms of violence. He went even further by arguing that knighthood was compatible with monasticism: the knights' duty was to kill for Christ and, in doing so, would rid the world of evil, not evil-doers. He argued that there was a difference between *homicide* – killing, which was a sin – and *malecide* – the killing of evil, which was not. Not only was it possible to gain Christ by dying for him, it was, according to Bernard, also possible to attain salvation by killing for him as well. A more concise argument in favour of holy war would be difficult to imagine.

Whatever criticisms the Order faced immediately after the triumph of Troyes, they did not seem to impede the willingness of nobles to help in the fight against the infidel. Baldwin's attack on Damascus in November 1129 comprised a number of Templars in addition to a great number of men whom Hugues had recruited during the European tour. The expedition got within six miles of Damascus before a breakaway contingent under William of Bures decided that the time was ripe for some pillaging. William lost control of the group, and they were attacked by Damascene cavalry. There were only 45 survivors. Baldwin hoped to catch the Damascenes off guard as they were celebrating their victory over the Franks, but as Baldwin's troops readied for an attack, the rains came down, making the roads so impassable that the offensive had to be called off.

The failure of the attack on Damascus did not seem to affect the Templars adversely. Donations, which throughout the Order's existence usually came in the form of grants of land and buildings (together with the people who lived there) and the right to receive the revenues from them, not only continued, but accelerated. Usually, the reasons for donations were to confirm the donor's piety, in the same way that rich merchants or worthies might commission the building of a chapel that would help exonerate their sins and stand them in good stead in the next world. The fight against the infidel was seen in the same terms, and the Templars found no shortage of penitents who wished to wipe their slates clean.

The most extensive donation came in October 1131, when the Templars – together with the other main military order, the Knights Hospitaller, and the Church of the Holy Sepulchre in Jerusalem – were left the entire Kingdom of Aragon in the will of its ruler, Alfonso I, 'The Battler'. Aragon under Alfonso had expanded rapidly since 1118, and the gains had been so great that Alfonso's resources were becoming increasingly stretched. The Iberian peninsula had been invaded by Muslim forces in 711, but the Christian counterattack, known as the *Reconquista*, began almost at once. When an alliance of Visigoths and Asturians defeated a Muslim army at Covadonga in 722, none of them could have known that the process of reclaiming the peninsula for Christ would take centuries of conflict.

Alfonso's response to maintaining his newly enlarged lands was to establish confraternities of knights to guard against any further Muslim reconquest, and the orders he established between 1122 and 1130, such as the orders of Belchite and Monreal del Campo, were similar to the Templars in that brothers served for a set time, but were not required to take monastic vows. The project was not entirely successful, however, as the Order of Monreal del Campo was on the verge of fizzling out by the time Alfonso drew up his will, with the result that the military orders of the East seemed to be the best solution to the problem. In addition, Alfonso was childless, which made securing the kingdom even more of a priority. Although Alfonso died in 1134, it took nine years for the will to be enforced, so enormous were the complexities of bequeathing such vast areas of land to so few beneficiaries. Although the Templars inherited somewhat less than Alfonso originally intended, they nonetheless were left with huge tracts of land across his former kingdom. From then on, the Templars would almost totally replace Alfonso's stillborn orders and become a major force in the *Reconquista* against the forces of Islam.

Shortly after Alfonso's death, the Templars began to receive castles in Outremer. The first were not in the Kingdom of Jerusalem at all, but north of Antioch in what was known as the Amanus March. This was a mountainous region that connected the Principality of Antioch with Cilician Armenia, and the Templars were given the task of guarding the Belen Pass. The first fortress they were given was Baghras, which they renamed Gaston, followed by Darbsaq, La Roche de Roussel and La Roche Guillaume. To the south-west of these strongholds was Port Bonnel, given to the Order at around the same time, which gave them access to the sea. In frontier regions such as the Amanus March, Templar properties such as Baghras were always fortified as they were places of high strategic value. Given the ever-unstable situation in the East, almost all Templar properties had some kind of fortification, whether they were castles or not. In the West, on the other hand, most Templar preceptories were not fortified, as they were not situated in potentially hostile areas (the exceptions being on the Iberian peninsula, where the threat of Moorish aggression was never far away, and also in eastern Europe, where the military orders campaigned against the indigenous pagans).

If the ever-increasing flow of money and property into the Temple's coffers was helping to alleviate doubts – both within and without the Order – about the purpose, effectiveness and morality of the Templars, then the three papal bulls (named after the *bullum*, or seal, used on the parchment) secured by Robert de Craon, the second Grand Master, raised the Order above any official reproach save that from the Papacy itself. It did not put an end to commentators criticising the Templars, but the bulls put them in a position where such comments were superfluous. Put simply, from 1139, just as they were establishing themselves in the Amanus March, the Templars, on something of a roll since the Council of Troyes, became untouchable.

Papal Approval: The Three Bulls

Robert de Craon, known as 'Robert the Burgundian', despite the fact that he was a native of Anjou, succeeded Hugues de Payen as Grand Master after the latter's death (which occurred on 24 May, probably in 1136). He was a skilful administrator, and knew that if the Order was ever to consolidate the gains made at Troyes, then nothing less than Papal privileges would secure them. Three years later, that is exactly what he secured from Pope Innocent II.

The bull *Omne datum optimum*, drawn up at the Lateran on 29 March 1139, made the Templars answerable to none save the Pontiff himself. The bull confirmed the Rule of the Order, and also all donations made to it. In addition, the workings of the Order were addressed: the Templars were allowed to elect their own Master without outside interference; only the Master could change the Order's customs and observances, although only after consulting the Chapter of Brothers (the Chapter was a sort of ruling council of each preceptory); the brothers were forbidden to give oaths of loyalty to anyone outside of the Order; and no professed brother was allowed to return to the secular world or join another order. The bull went on to exempt the Templars from paying tithes, but allowed them to receive them from clergy and laity alike, provided that the tithes were presented as gifts freely given (a privilege that had previously only applied to the Cistercians).

Aside from allowing the Order to keep all booty captured

from the Muslims, the remainder of the bull was concerned with
the Order's spiritual life. The Templars could receive clerks and
priests to serve the Order, but first needed the consent of the
priest's bishop. If the bishop refused, he could be overruled by
the Pope himself. The Order retained the right to remove a
priest if he caused disturbances within the Order or proved
himself to be more of a hindrance than an asset, provided that
the Chapter approved. However, a priest might be allowed to
join the Order after he had served for one year, if the brothers
approved. The priests would not be called upon to fight, but to
have care of the brothers' souls only. The priests would not be
subject to anyone from outside the Order, and the Templars had
the right to have their clergy ordained by any bishop.
Furthermore, the Order's clergy were not allowed to preach for
money, unless by prior arrangement with the Master. The
Templars were to be allowed to build oratories on their land, and
be permitted to hear divine office there. Serving brothers could
be buried there when they died. Wherever they travelled, the
brothers could hear confession from any priest, and receive any
sacrament or unction. The privileges set out in *Omne datum
optimum* also covered the Templars' household and servants. The
bull ended with Innocent quoting 1 Corinthians, Chapter 7,
Verse 20: 'each of you to remain in that vocation to which you
are called'.

The privileges granted to the Templars by Innocent were
reinforced by his successors, Celestine II and Eugenius III. *Milites
Templi*, issued by Celestine in 1144, was addressed to the clergy.
In this, the Templars were described as defending pilgrims and
protecting the Church from the pagans; as a result, the clergy
were ordered to make a collection for the Templars. Celestine
urged donors to form confraternities to support the Order, and
whosoever joined one would have one-seventh of his penance

remitted. As a further perk, members of the confraternities would have the right to be buried in churches unless they had been excommunicated. When the Templars came to collect the confraternity's money, the churches would be opened on one day a year for that purpose only, and the offices heard. *Militia Dei*, issued the following year, was again addressed to the clergy, and gave the Templars further privileges. Eugenius promised not to damage their rights, and announced that the Templars had permission to take on priests for their Order. The priests needed to be properly ordained and have their bishop's permission before they could serve the Order. The brothers could take tithes and burial offerings where they had a house, and could build oratories and bury their brothers and servants when they died. Eugenius asked the clergy to consecrate Templar oratories, bless their cemeteries and allow their priests to work in peace.

The three bulls legitimised the Templars and firmly established them at the heart of Christendom's efforts in the Holy Land. Although criticism of the Order was to continue, there was little any critic could do; the Templars were above reproach. It had been a remarkable ascendancy – from the Council of Troyes, the Templars had gone from being a slightly shady organisation of unknown provenance to being the defenders of the one true faith in a mere 15 years. For the next century and a half, their position would remain unassailable; few could have predicted that their eventual fall would be as meteorically swift as their rise.

A Church within a Church,
a State within a State
(1145–1291)

The Second Crusade

The Second Crusade (1147–49) provided a measure of how successfully the Templars had established themselves in the years after the Council of Troyes and the three great bulls of privilege. On Christmas Eve 1144, the city of Edessa fell to an army under the command of Imad ad-Din Zengi, the *Atabeg* (governor) of Mosul and Aleppo. When news finally reached Pope Eugenius III the following autumn, he immediately wrote to King Louis VII of France, imploring him to lead a new crusade to rescue Edessa from the infidel. Louis was not at all popular in France at the time, as three years earlier he had started a war when he illegally seized lands belonging to his most powerful vassal, Theobald of Champagne, and he seems to have been surprised when none of his barons showed much interest in his proposal for a new expedition to the East. It was decided that the matter would be settled at a meeting at Vézelay in Burgundy at Easter 1146. Realising that he was potentially without allies, Louis turned to the one man who had the clout to rally would-be crusaders, and that was Bernard of Clairvaux.

The scene at Vézelay on 31 March 1146 was reminiscent of Clermont in 1095 – huge crowds had gathered, drawn by the prospect of hearing Bernard preach the crusade. So many had arrived in Vézelay that Bernard had to deliver his sermon from a specially constructed platform on the outskirts of town. Bernard's words found a receptive audience. As soon as he had finished speaking, King Louis was the first to pledge allegiance, followed by his brother Robert, the Count of Dreux. Of all those who vowed to journey to the East that day, many were the sons and grandsons of the original crusaders, to whom maintaining family honour was at least as important as liberating Edessa. Bernard later wrote to King Louis of the success of Vézelay: 'Villages and towns are now deserted... Everywhere you will see widows whose husbands are still alive.'[9]

On 27 April 1147, a Chapter meeting of the Paris Temple welcomed both King Louis and Pope Eugenius in the build-up to the crusade's departure. Also present were four archbishops, 130 Templar knights and at least as many Templar sergeants and squires. Eugenius appointed Aymar, the Templar treasurer, to receive the tax that he had imposed on all Church goods to finance the crusade. William of Tyre, the great chronicler who was writing a generation later, believed that it was at this meeting that the Pope conferred on the Templars the right to wear a red cross on their white mantles, which symbolised their willingness to suffer martyrdom in defending the Holy Land against the infidel.

Germany was fermenting with crusading zeal by this time, after King Conrad III had heard Bernard preach in the Rhineland. Eugenius had originally wanted Conrad to help in the fight against his primary foe, the Norman king, Roger of Sicily, but as Conrad could not be dissuaded from going on crusade, it was decided that he should lead a German force that would work alongside the French.

Everard des Barres, Master of the Temple in France, together with the knights present at the April Chapter meeting, accompanied the French army under Louis on the overland route taken by the First Crusade. Everard proved himself to be one of Louis' most trusted advisors, and the French king sent the Templar Master ahead to Constantinople to negotiate the Crusade's passage through Byzantine territory. Unlike his predecessor Alexius, the Byzantine Emperor Manuel Comnenus had not asked for Western help, and was somewhat nervous at the prospect of the crusading force (made up largely of the French and German armies) bearing down upon his lands. Everard succeeded in getting the Crusaders through, although Manuel was looked upon with grave suspicion by the Franks, as he had signed a peace treaty with the Seljuk Turks in order to wage war against Roger of Sicily. Manuel was equally uneasy with the crusaders, and was glad to see the back of them.

In January 1148, the Crusade got into further difficulty. Demoralised by severe weather and the news that Conrad's army – which had gone ahead of the French – had suffered a defeat at Dorylaeum by the Seljuk Turks, the French came under attack in the narrow passes of the Cadmus mountains. The Franks' heavy cavalry was useless in such terrain, and the columns of crusaders came under constant attack from the Turkish light infantry, whose archers were masters of firing from the saddle. The Franks were further hampered by an acute shortage of horses and provisions, and it seemed as though the Crusade would be over before it ever reached Outremer. Once again, Louis turned to Everard des Barres and the Templars. Everard broke the army up into units of 50, each under the command of a Templar, who in turn were answerable to another Templar knight, Brother Gilbert. This provided the beleaguered French with sufficient morale and order to continue as far as the Byzantine port of Attalia, where Louis took his best troops by boat to Antioch.

At Antioch, the Crusade took yet another turn for the worse. Louis had all but exhausted his funds in getting the army across

Asia Minor; once again, Everard des Barres was the man to whom Louis turned for help. On 10 May, Everard sailed from Antioch to Acre, where he raised sufficient capital to fund the rest of the crusade, either by drawing directly from the treasury at the Templar preceptory in Acre, or by borrowing, using the Order's possessions as security. Whichever was the case, it proved that the Templars had become a major financial institution, and it cemented the relationship between the Order and the French crown, with the result that the Templars effectively became the French royal treasury until the late thirteenth century.

The Templars seem to have played a less prominent role in the remainder of the crusade. A council of war was convened at Acre in June to decide on a course of action, with the Templar Grand Master Robert de Craon present, together with the Grand Master of the Hospital, Raymond du Puy. After debating whether they should head for Edessa via Aleppo, or whether they should instead strike out for Ascalon in the south, it was eventually decided that the target should be Damascus, which the crusaders planned to attack the following month. After initial success in besieging the city from the west, the crusaders made the tactical blunder of decamping to a position on the east of the city. Unlike their original position, which had been well supplied, this new eastern position had no water and also faced the best fortified section of the city walls. With rumours that a huge Muslim army under Zengi's son Nur ed-Din (Zengi having died in 1146) was on its way, the crusaders lost their nerve and retreated. The Second Crusade was over, and the recriminations for its failure began.

There were various theories as to why the Second Crusade had been such a fiasco. Accusations of treachery abounded, with various parties being named as the chief culprits. The crusaders, unused to life in the East, were shocked by the way Christians in Outremer had assimilated Eastern ways, and the 'Men of Jerusalem', as they were called, were seen as the guilty party by a number of commentators in the West. John of Würzburg, a German monk who travelled to Outremer in the 1160s, believed that the Crusade's failure was due to Templar treachery. John's anonymous colleague, known as the Würzburg Annalist, went even further, and stated that the Templars had been paid off by the Damascenes to lift the siege. Only later was it found that the money the Orders had been paid was in fact counterfeit, which was seen as Divine punishment for betraying the Christian cause. Other variants of the story had the 'Men of Jerusalem' accepting the money, while the early thirteenth-century chronicle of Ernoul and Bernard the Treasurer had the Hospitallers working alongside the Templars in putting profit before God. However, the Military Orders' sternest critic of the time, William of Tyre, does not mention either the Templars or the Hospitallers in connection with the failure of the Crusade. As the bad press the orders received dates from several decades later, it would seem that the chroniclers were reflecting contemporary disillusion with both the Temple and the Hospital and projecting it back to 1148.

Given that the Templars played a major role in financing the Second Crusade, it might be worth examining the role the Order played in the financial affairs of both Outremer and the West, and the subsequent dominance they exerted over what was to evolve into a system of international banking.

The Temple as Bankers

The Templars quite early on in their history developed a reputation for being reliable bankers. They were – in effect – Europe's first bank. They developed a system of credit notes whereby money deposited in one Templar preceptory could be withdrawn at another upon production of a credit note. Monies thus deposited proved to be quite safe, as Templar keeps were formidable buildings. Some of their castles in Outremer, for instance, were so well defended that they were impregnable (such as their massive fortress at 'Atlit, which was actually a fortified peninsula rather than a mere castle). In Europe, the imposing edifice of the Paris Temple became their financial base (as did, to a lesser extent, the London Temple).

Louis VII was the first of a number of European monarchs whose finances were saved from collapse by Templar loans, although the size of the loan that the Templars provided brought the Order close to bankruptcy. It is thought that the Order provided him with 2,000 marks of silver and 30,000 *livres parisis*. The magnitude of this amount of money can be seen when it is compared to revenues from French royal lands which, even 20 or so years after the Second Crusade, were only about 60,000 *livres parisis* per year.

Louis VII was not the only French monarch who was to become reliant on the Order's financial services. The Second Crusade saw the beginning of a long association between the Order and the kings of France. By the reign of Philip II (1180–1223), the Templars were effectively the French royal treasury. During the course of his reign, they increased the revenues from royal estates by 120 per cent, and were heavily involved in Philip's restructuring of Capetian finances. During the thirteenth century, the Templar treasurer in Paris was always a man selected by the king, and the treasurers became trusted advisers to Philip and his successors. When Louis' great-grandson, Louis IX, was held hostage after the disasters of the Seventh Crusade in 1250, it was to the Temple that the French commanders looked for the remaining 30,000 *livres* that they required to bail him out (although, on this occasion the Templar commander, Stephen of Otricourt, was less than happy to comply).

That the Templars proved themselves to be so successful as bankers is due in no large part to the meticulousness of their records, and their objectivity in dealing with clients. Records survive from the Paris Temple for the period 12 March 1295 to 4 July the following year, and they give a clear indication of how busy the Paris Temple was in its role as banker. These records — eight surviving sheets of parchment — record the date and the Templar on duty at the time, in addition to the amount deposited, by whom, into which account the money should be paid and from where the amount came from. At the end of each day, the receipts collected would be taken to the strong rooms to be deposited. (During the 1260s and 1270s, a great tower was built in order to house the various monies the Order was keeping.) There were more than 60 active accounts at the Paris Temple during this period, with the account holders being a mixture of royalty, clergy, important nobles and Templar officials. No business was done at Christmas, Easter and Ascension, and also on the Feast Days of saints who had a particular relevance for the Order, such as John the Baptist. Outside of these dates, the hours the Temple was open for business depended largely on the needs of its clients. In August 1295, for instance, they were only open for six days, whereas that December, they were far busier, being at one point open on 11 consecutive days. The Paris Temple also sent out statements to important clients several times a year, detailing the movements within their accounts.

Matters did not always go smoothly, however, as the chronicler Joinville discovered to his cost on the Seventh Crusade.

While the army was recuperating at Acre following King Louis' ransom, Joinville received 400 *livres* in wages. He kept 40 and deposited the remaining 360 with the Templars. When he sent one of his men to withdraw another 40 for current living expenses, the Templar treasurer denied all knowledge of Joinville and his savings. Joinville then complained to the newly elected Grand Master, Reginald de Vichiers, who was initially dubious at Joinville's accusation that the treasurer had lost his money. Reginald looked into the matter, and several days later was able to report to a much relieved Joinville that his money had been found; the treasurer was transferred out of Acre.

The Papacy also came to be dependent on the Templars for its financial needs. The Templars were acting as Pope Alexander III's (1159–81) bankers from as early as 1163, and, as they had been involved with the overhaul of Capetian finances under Philip II, so the Order was also used by Pope Innocent III when he undertook to reorganise crusading finances at the time of the Fourth Crusade (1202–4). A new tax, levied on the clergy for the express purpose of being used to fund the campaigns in the East, was to be paid into Templar and Hospitaller preceptories; the military orders would then be responsible for transporting the money safely to the Holy Land. A similar procedure was followed by Honorius III when he was raising funds for the Fifth Crusade (1218–21), with the money raised to be transferred to the papal legate in Egypt.

Kings from other countries likewise came to the Temple. The kings of Aragon were heavy borrowers, and King Henry II of England (1154–89) used the Order to accumulate crusading funds in Jerusalem, whilst his son King John (1199–1216) was borrowing anything from nine marks of gold for an offering to be made when he was absolved following the lifting of his excommunication in 1213, to loans of over 4,000 marks two years later to pay the wages of troops in Poitou and Gascony. During his wars with the barons, John's son Henry III (1216–72) moved the crown jewels to the Paris Temple for safekeeping in 1261, where they were inventoried and stored until further notice. The further notice duly came three years later, when Henry used them as security on a loan to finance further campaigns against the barons.

The Templars' financial services were not restricted to providing loans, however, and not just for the royalty and nobility. As crusaders and pilgrims might be away from Europe for several years, the Templars also accepted precious documents and objects for safekeeping, including wills. One such example was the will of Pierre Sarrasin, which was drawn up in June 1220 before he set out for Santiago de Compostella. In it, he specified that, if he failed to return, the Templars should pay 600 *livres parisis* to the Abbey of St Victor, and that this should be used to buy rents from corn, the annual proceeds from which (about 200 *livres parisis*) were to be used to make daily donations of bread; furthermore, there were additional beneficiaries, including his mother, who was to be paid 100 *livres*. The remainder of the estate was to be held by the Templars until Pierre's heirs came of age.

The Structure of the Order

As the Temple grew from being the original nine soldier-monks sworn to poverty, chastity and obedience into what we would nowadays recognise as a multinational corporation, so too did the structure of the Order evolve to reflect and support its expanding role in the affairs of the crusader states.

The Grand Master was the absolute ruler over the Order; after the bull *Omne datum optimum* of 1139 he was answerable only to the Pope. Grand Masters were chosen by an electoral college of 13 senior Templars, comprising eight knights, four sergeants and one chaplain. Generally, the electoral college would try to choose someone who was already based in the East. Given the importance of the Paris Temple to the French monarchy, French kings could – and often did – influence the choice of a Grand Master, such as during the election of Reginald de Vichiers in 1250. As the Order expanded, so did the trappings of office: by the time of Bertrand de Blancfort's tenure (1156–69), a Grand Master could expect to have four horses, and an entourage made up of two knights, a sergeant, a chaplain, a turcopolier, a farrier, a cook and a Saracen secretary. The Master also had first choice whenever the Order received a fresh batch of horses from the West.

Immediately beneath the Grand Master was a Chapter of senior officials. The Seneschal was both deputy and adviser to the Grand Master. On occasion, Seneschals would eventually become 'promoted' to Grand Master – the politics of the electoral college permitting – such as André de Montbard, who was one of Hugues de Payen's original knights. After acting as Seneschal for four years, he finally became Grand Master in 1153 after the short Mastership of Bernard de Tremelay had come to an abrupt and bloody end at Ascalon. Like the Grand Master, the Seneschal also had his own staff. The Marshal was responsible for all military decisions, such as the purchase of horses and equipment, and also had jurisdiction over the regional commanders. These were commanders who had responsibility for one specific area: the Commander of the Kingdom of Jerusalem acted as the Order's treasurer, oversaw the Kingdom and had the same powers as the Grand Master within it; the Commander of the City of Jerusalem, who likewise was overlord of the city only, also had the same powers as the Grand Master within its walls; and the commanders of Tripoli, Acre and Antioch were invested with similar powers. Each major kingdom in the West with a significant Templar presence had a Master who was answerable to the Grand Master: France, England, Aragon, Portugal, Poitou, Apulia and Hungary. The Draper was responsible for the issue of clothing and bedding, and made sure that individual brothers did not hoard private property. He was also authorised to distribute gifts made to the Order.

There were further roles that seem to have been subservient to the various masters and commanders. The Commander of Houses was responsible for specific Templar houses in the East and was answerable to the higher ranks; the Commander of Knights acted as deputy to the Commander of the Kingdom of Jerusalem; the Turcopolier was in charge of the turcopoles (the light cavalry who were often local troops engaged for a fixed period); the Under Marshal oversaw the footmen and the equipment; the Standard Bearer, usually a sergeant, was responsible for the conduct of the squires; while the Infirmarer looked after sick and aged brothers, who would often be sent back to reside in the Order's Western houses, away from the front lines of Outremer and the Iberian Peninsula.

The elite of the Templar fighting force was comprised of the group perhaps most readily pictured when we think of the Order – the knights with their white mantles bearing the distinctive red cross over the heart. They would already be expected to be skilled in the arts of war before joining the Order, when they would hand over their secular clothes and be issued with armour, equipment and clothing to wear when not in the field. Although originally knights could be from any social group (including excommunicates, such was the constant need for manpower in the East), by the time of the Second Crusade it was necessary for knights to be descended from knightly stock.

Each knight would be granted three horses and a squire, whose role would be to assist the knight and to make sure that he was fully equipped and ready to go into battle. Like the turcopoles, squires were usually not fully sworn-in Templars, but often locals who were hired for a set period.

The other main group of fighting Templars was the sergeants, who, unlike the knights, wore black or brown mantles, and were not as heavily armed. Sergeants were from a much more socially and racially mixed background than the knights, and their ranks were often made up with men of Armenian and Syrian origin. They had to make do with only one horse, and were required to be their own squires.

Gaza and Ascalon

Despite the major setback of the Second Crusade, the Christian presence in Outremer continued to be pre-emptive. The one coastal city that remained in Muslim hands was Ascalon, and a series of forts had been built around it to hem it in. During the winter of 1149–50, King Baldwin III gave the Templars Gaza, which lay a dozen or so miles to the south. The city was largely in ruins, and the Templars set about rebuilding the fort – it was the first important castle the Order received in the Kingdom of Jerusalem. The Egyptian forces, now unable to supply Ascalon by land, tried to retake Gaza almost as soon as the Templars had acquired the city; the attempt failed.

The siege of Ascalon finally began on 25 January 1153, and the campaign reached its climax during the summer. On the night of 15 August, a sortie of defenders from the city set fire to the Franks' mobile siege tower. The wind changed direction, however, and blew the flames back against the city walls. The ensuing fire caused part of the wall to collapse, and a Templar contingent under the Grand Master, Bernard de Tremelay, rushed into the breach. The chronicler William of Tyre records that Bernard forbade non-Templars to enter the city, such was the Templar greed for booty. They made an unsuccessful stand in the city; the next day, their beheaded bodies were hung over the walls of Ascalon. No Muslim source records this incident, and it is possible that William was venting his habitual ire; rather than a desire for booty, Bernard and his men may have simply perished trying to hold open the breach in the wall. Either way, the city fell a week later, and the Templars' reputation for avarice had begun.

The Templars in the West

What had seemed, to commentators in both Outremer and the West, to be an avaricious streak in the Order of the Temple was, in many cases, merely a misunderstanding of the fact that the Order ran its estates with scrupulous care. The land donated to them in the West since Hugues de Payen's visit of 1127–29 formed the basis of the Order's wealth. As Malcolm Barber has noted, 'without an extensive network of support in the West, the Templars would have vanished with the first major defeat they suffered'.[10] This network took the form of their European preceptories, which were initially acquired through the extensive programme of donations that transpired during and after Hugues de Payen's tour.

Ordinarily, a Templar preceptory would be an estate (a farm or a manor, for instance) that would then develop a network of daughter houses around it. All the revenues from both the mother and daughter houses would be directed towards campaigning in the East. A tax, known as the *responsion*, was raised, whereby one-third of all revenues collected from a Templar house in the West was to be used to support the Order's work in the Holy Land. These Western houses were generally established in all the main cities, financial centres and ports of Europe. Wherever there was trade, there were Templars.

The preceptories not only kept the Order bankrolled, but also supplied food, clothes, arms and horses. This, together with the Templars' increasingly important role in the East, meant that the work of the Western houses was even more vital in keeping the Order freshly supplied. With rising prices in the thirteenth century, the onus was on the preceptories to maintain a permanent vigilance over their accounts, and to be constantly on the lookout for new ways to make money. Thus, the Order's holdings expanded to include not just farmland, but also wine presses, orchards and even tile factories. To gain further support, the Templars introduced a kind of affiliate membership whereby one could, after a donation, hear Mass in a Templar church and have the right to burial in a Templar cemetery. In some cases, the Templars provided these donors with a pension if there was no one else to look after them.

The majority of the Templars' 9,000 Western manors were in France, and, to a lesser extent, Italy. While the Order had property in Germany, that country was largely the province of the Teutonic Knights. Likewise, on the Iberian Peninsula, the Templars – although heavily involved in the *Reconquista* – generally had a lower profile than that of the great Spanish and Portuguese orders, Calatrava, Santiago and Alcántara. In England, the Order's base was at the London Temple, with its holdings being scattered across the country, from Penzance and the island of Lundy in the Bristol Channel to Yorkshire and Lincolnshire. (Generally speaking, any modern English place name that has the prefix of 'Temple' was once owned by the Order.) The Order also had substantial land holdings in Scotland and Ireland, establishing regional headquarters at Balantradoch and Clontarf respectively.

The Temple and the Crescent Moon

One of the reasons why the Second Crusade was seen to have failed was perfidy on the part of the 'Men of Jerusalem' and the Military Orders. The Crusaders under Louis VII had been shocked at how much the Latins in Outremer had adopted Eastern ways, unaware that in many cases the adoption of local custom was the most pragmatic thing to do. The culture of the Arab world was more refined than the culture most Crusaders had known in the West:

> 'The Franks employed Syrian doctors, cooks, servants, artisans, labourers. They clothed themselves in Eastern garments, included in their diets the fruits and dishes of the country. They had glass in their windows, mosaics on their floors, fountains in the courtyards of their houses, which were planned on the Syrian model. They had dancing girls at their entertainments; professional mourners at their funerals; took baths; used soap; ate sugar.'[11]

In addition, the Franks in Outremer had fresh produce all year round, including fruit and vegetables that were unknown in Europe, such as peaches, olives and bananas.

There were more serious practicalities, however. Although Jerusalem was in Christian hands, the majority of the population were still Muslim. They remained second-class citizens unless they converted, but were allowed to choose their own community leaders and, as long as they paid their taxes on time, their Christian rulers were content to let them be. Similarly, the Jewish community remained relatively unharassed (which was in remarkable contrast to the atrocities committed against both communities during the First Crusade).

The Templars showed a great deal of tolerance towards Islam.

As has been noted, Grand Masters always had Saracen secretaries, and it was not uncommon for Templars to learn Arabic. One Muslim ambassador visiting the Templars in Jerusalem was given a small chapel in which to pray; when a Frank tried to stop him, the Templars dragged the man off and let the ambassador say his prayers to Mecca in peace.

One group with whom the Templars had a less convivial relationship was the Assassins. They were a fanatical sect of Shi'ite Muslims, who had broken away in the late eleventh century from the Fatimids, the dominant Shi'ite caliphate, and set themselves up in the Elburz mountains in northern Persia and later in the mountains of the Lebanon; their leader became known to the Franks as 'the Old Man of the Mountains'. The Shi'ites were strongly messianic and mystical, believing in the coming of the Mahdi, 'the Guided One', who would appear to destroy tyranny and establish Paradise. They pursued their goals through an unpredictable campaign of terror in which Assassin killers would murder their opponents in audacious – sometimes suicidal – attacks. (Their name derives from *hashishim*, an ingester of hashish. The drug was said to make the taker oblivious to danger.) Frequently, these victims were Muslims from the main rival sect of Islam, the Sunnis, or even other Shi'ite groups.

In 1173, the King of Jerusalem, Amalric I (1162–74), attempted to negotiate an alliance with the Assassins, as Amalric was given to believe that the Old Man of the Mountains was about to convert to Christianity. This was perhaps not as ludicrous as it may sound, as the Old Man had, just a few years earlier, abrogated the law of the Prophet and proclaimed the Millennium, thus making himself and the rest of the sect heretical. The Templars were less certain about the Old Man's threatened apostasy, and a group of Templar knights ambushed Abdullah, the Old Man's envoy, near Tripoli and killed him.

Amalric was furious, and commentators such as William of Tyre and Walter Map seized upon the opportunity to launch another attack on the greed of the Temple: in their view, the Order was afraid of losing its annual tribute of 2,000 *besants* that the Assassins paid to the Templars to leave them largely alone. The Grand Master, Odo de St Amand, refused to hand over the killer, a one-eyed knight by the name of Walter of Mesnil, saying that Innocent's great bull of 1139 put the Templars above the jurisdiction of the throne of Jerusalem, and he would instead send Walter to Rome to be dealt with. Amalric ignored this and seized Walter at Sidon, where the Templar chapter was in session, and had him cast into prison. Amalric managed to persuade the Old Man that the Templars had been acting on their own, but all attempts at forging an alliance with the Assassins were dropped.

The incident showed that, if need be, the Templars would not only go against a Muslim group who, if not actual allies, were at least tolerated and accorded some degree of respect, but also the King of Jerusalem himself. A reason for the murder has never been fully established. That the Templars were afraid of losing their tribute is unlikely, given the wealth of the Order by this time; perhaps they knew only too well that the Assassins could not be entirely trusted, and a breakaway Templar faction under Walter of Mesnil decided to take matters into its own hands.

The Temple as Architects

The Affair of the Assassin Envoy, as it came to be known, shows how far the Order had become independent of all authority save that of the Pope himself, and detractors, railing against the privileges that the Templars enjoyed, accused them of having become 'a church within a church, a state within a state'. Such criticism appeared to have no effect on the Order, however, and, if the Templars' building programme in the East is any indicator, it probably only reinforced their belief that they were different because it was the will of God.

Templar masons built a number of churches throughout the Crusader states, and were involved in several major projects, including the construction of the new Church of the Holy Sepulchre, dedicated in 1149, and the renovation of the Church of the Nativity in Bethlehem. In addition, they provided an elaborate tomb for Baldwin IV, the leper king, upon his death in 1185. Their churches and buildings in the West tended to be simpler, with major expense being reserved for important preceptories such as Paris and London. Likewise, not all their churches boasted the distinctive round design, such as the Temple Church in London. (The round churches were apparently inspired by the Church of the Holy Sepulchre in Jerusalem.) Regional preceptories, such as Temple Garway in Herefordshire, were simple, austere but functional places.

The other major feat of Templar architecture in the East was the fortresses they either reinforced, rebuilt or had constructed especially for them. Castles such as Safad in Galilee, Tortosa in the County of Tripoli and 'Atlit on the coast south of Haifa were masterpieces of mediaeval military architecture. Indeed, so strong were the fortifications at 'Atlit – its outer walls were 15ft (4.5m) thick – that it even managed to withstand a major assault while it was still being built.

The Templars had, in fact, been closely involved with building projects since their inception. When King Baldwin II had moved out of the al-Aqsa mosque around 1120, the Templars were given free reign to develop the area as they saw fit. Theoderich, a German monk who visited the Holy Land between 1169 and 1174, wrote a detailed account of the Temple area:

'One follows to the south [from the Dome of the Rock, rechristened the Temple of the Lord after the First Crusade], and there is the Palace of Solomon [al-Aqsa]. Like a church it is oblong and supported by pillars, and also at the end of the sanctuary it rises up to a circular roof, large and round, and also like a church. This and all its neighbouring buildings have come into the possession of the Templar soldiers. They are garrisoned in these and other buildings belonging to them. And with stores of arms, clothing and food they are always ready to guard the province and defend it. Below them they have stables once erected by King Solomon. They are next to the Palace, and their structure is remarkably complex. They are erected with vaults, arches and roofs of many varieties, and according to our estimation we should bear witness that they will hold ten thousand horses with their grooms. A single shot from a cross-bow would hardly reach from one end of this building to the other, either in length or breadth.

'Above them the area is full of houses, dwellings and outbuildings for every kind of purpose, and it is full of walking-places, lawns, council-chambers, porches, consistories and supplies of water in splendid cisterns. Below it is equally full of washrooms, stores, grain rooms, stores for wood and other kinds of domestic stores.

'On the other side of the Palace, that is on the West, the Templars have built a new house, whose height, length and breadth, and all its cellars and refectories, staircase and roof, are far beyond the custom of this land. Indeed its roof is so high that, if I were to mention how high it is, those who listen would hardly believe me. There indeed they have constructed a new Palace, just as on the other side they have the old one. There too they have founded on the edge of the outer court a new church of magnificent size and workmanship.'[12]

Given that the area around the southern end of the Temple platform was in need of some repair when Baldwin vacated it, and given the extent of the Templar work carried out there, the

Order would seem to have been busy, probably from almost the time they moved in. When Theoderich saw it, the Temple area was at its most developed. But, unbeknown to him, the Order's time there was limited and the new church he saw being built would never be completed.

The Loss of Jerusalem

Coming after the disaster of the Second Crusade, the fall of Ascalon can be seen as one of the high points of twelfth-century crusader campaigning. For the remainder of the 1150s and into the 1160s, the situation between Franks and Muslims would remain in something of a stalemate, seeing tit-for-tat raiding on both sides, with the Templars playing a crucial part in Christian campaigns. However, a series of events transpired in the 1160s that led the Templars to favour ploughing their own furrow when it came to matters of military tactics.

King Baldwin III died at the age of 33 in 1162 and was succeeded by his brother, the 25-year-old Amalric. Amalric's gaze was firmly fixed on Egypt and, in the autumn of 1163, he launched a campaign against Cairo. Egypt, at the time weakened by political chaos, was seen as a fabulous prize by both Amalric and Nur ed-Din, and each was keen that it should not fall into the hands of the other. The Templars, as usual, participated in the campaign under their Grand Master, Bertrand de Blancfort, but the Egyptians forced the Franks back by breaching the dykes in the Nile Delta. Amalric was not to be kept out of Egypt for long, and he returned the following year. Whilst Amalric was negotiating with Shawar, the Egyptian vizier, Nur ed-Din attacked Antioch. With Amalric unable to return, a force led by Prince Bohemond III, which included a Templar contingent, confronted Nur ed-Din's much larger forces on 10 August 1164. Against the advice of nearly everyone – including the Templars – Bohemond ordered an attack. The Franks were routed, with 60 Templar knights perishing; only seven escaped.

Relations between the Temple and the King of Jerusalem soured even further two years later when a Templar cave-fortress in Transjordan was besieged by Nur ed-Din's troops. Amalric and his forces rushed to relieve the Templars only to meet 12 Templar knights as they were coming back across the River Jordan. The Templars explained that they had been involved in the siege and had surrendered the fortress to the Muslims. Amalric was so incensed that he ordered the Templars to be hanged. When Amalric mounted a full-scale invasion of Egypt in the autumn of 1168, the Templars refused to take part.

As has been noted earlier, the Affair of the Assassin Envoy, coming five years after the Templars' absence from the Egyptian campaign, further strained relations between the Order and the King. The following year, Amalric died. So too did Nur ed-Din. Both rulers' heirs were minors, with Amalric's son being the 13-year-old leper, Baldwin IV, while Nur ed-Din's son Malik was only 11. This led to rival claims from the *atabegs* of Damascus, Aleppo, Mosul and Cairo, and it was from Cairo that Outremer's greatest adversary emerged.

Salad ed-Din Yusuf, more commonly known as Saladin, had been one of the Muslim generals who had played a prominent part in keeping Amalric's forces at bay during the Egyptian campaigns of the 1160s, and he was to come into his own after Nur ed-Din's death by forging alliances and creating unity between the various Muslim kingdoms with the intention of continuing the *jihad* (holy war) against the Franks. As a young man, he had been more drawn towards religion, but came to feel that only a holy war would drive out the Franks, and so he became a master swordsman. Like most Muslim rulers of the time, he was also highly cultured and developed a reputation for both piety and mercy towards his enemies. Although he had his opponents within the Islamic world, he was respected by both Muslim and Christian alike, and he admired the fighting prowess of the Frankish knights. However, there was one segment of the Frankish population that he felt outright hatred for, perhaps because he understood how fanatical they were in their commitment to the Christian cause – he detested, possibly even feared, the military orders.

It was not long before the Templars engaged with forces under Saladin's control. In 1177, Saladin launched an attack against Gaza. The Templars were waiting for him. However, at the last minute, Saladin changed tack and laid siege to Ascalon instead. Baldwin IV, who had now come of age, led a counterattack. With Frankish forces concentrated at Ascalon and Gaza, Saladin, in a move reminiscent of Nur ed-Din's attack on Antioch, now decided that the relatively undefended Jerusalem would be his best option. Baldwin realised what Saladin was doing and, together with a Templar contingent from Gaza, raced after the Muslim army. They caught up with Saladin's forces at Montgisard on 25 November 1177 and destroyed them; Saladin evaded capture and escaped back to Egypt.

If Montgisard had confirmed Saladin's fear of the military might of the Templars, then the events of the summer of 1179 would show him their fanatical side. Acquiescing to pressure from the Templars, who recognised it to be a strategically important area on the road to Damascus, Baldwin had constructed a castle at Jacob's Ford on the Jordan; it was said to be the place where, according to the book of Genesis, Jacob had wrestled the angel.[13] Saladin besieged the castle, and on 10 June Templar forces under their Grand Master, Odo de St Amand, and a Christian army under Raymond of Tripoli, engaged Saladin's men. The Franks came off worse, and a number of knights were taken captive, among them Odo de St Amand. Normally, such a high-ranking Frankish noble would have been used as a bargaining tool, as had Bertrand de Blancfort when he had been captured by Nur ed-Din soon after becoming Templar Grand Master in 1156. He had been held captive for almost two years, and was released as part of a treaty signed between Byzantine Emperor Manuel Comnenus and Nur ed-Din. Odo, however, refused outright to be exchanged for a Muslim captive held by the Franks, and died in prison in 1180.

Odo's successor, Arnold of Torroja, had been Master in Spain and Provence since 1167, and was an experienced mediator. He tried to bring together the various factions in the East, knowing full well that if the Christians were split by internal disagreement, then their military strength would be fatally sapped. Saladin, a shrewd politician as well as a great commander in the field, was equally aware of potential haemorrhages amongst the Franks, and continued to consolidate his position with strategic alliances during the early 1180s, waiting for the time when Frankish disunity would signal the moment to attack. In 1184, Arnold set off for Europe with Roger des Moulins, Grand Master of the Hospital, and Patriarch Heraclius in an attempt to impress upon Western leaders the gravity of the threat posed by Saladin. Unfortunately, Arnold died before the embassy got under way, expiring at Verona on 30 September 1184, leaving Heraclius and Roger to continue the mission alone.

The man who succeeded Arnold of Torroja as Grand Master of the Temple, Gerard de Ridefort, had a reputation for rashness that exceeded even that of Odo de St Amand. He was of Flemish or Anglo-Norman origin, and was said to have joined the Order to get over a failed relationship; by 1179 he was Marshal of Jerusalem, and by 1183 he was acting as Seneschal. He was elected as Grand Master of the Temple probably in early 1185, around the time that Baldwin IV's leprosy finally killed him at the age of 24. Despite having had a somewhat strained relationship with the monarchy since the time of Amalric, the Temple under Gerard became closely involved with the succession issue; disastrously, as it turned out.

Baldwin was succeeded by his seven-year-old nephew, who reigned as Baldwin V, with Raymond of Tripoli acting as regent, and it was in his capacity as regent that Raymond, in an attempt to gain some stability and breathing space for Outremer, agreed a truce of four years with Saladin. The boy lasted a year before he too died. Under the conditions of the leper king's 1183 will, if his nephew were to die before he reached the age of ten, then Raymond of Tripoli would continue to act as regent while a new ruler was sought by the Pope, the Holy Roman Emperor and the kings of France and England. The will, however, did not foresee the coup of September 1186 that installed Sibyl, Baldwin IV's sister, on the throne of Jerusalem as queen to her husband Guy of Lusignan's king. Chief among the conspirators that effected Guy's accession to the throne of Jerusalem was Gerard de Ridefort. The Master of the Hospital, Roger des Moulins, was less enthusiastic about this weak minor French noble assuming the mantle of King of Jerusalem. The strongbox where the crown was kept was under two locks and two keys, each key being held by the Masters of the Temple and the Hospital, and it is said that on coronation day, when it was time for the strongbox to be opened in order to crown Guy, Roger threw his key out of the window, forcing Gerard to go outside to look for it.[14]

Guy was instantly unpopular. He was a weak king, who was seen by many of Outremer's vassals as being a usurper. His acceptance of the throne seriously exacerbated the factionalism among the Franks – which had played a part in his accession in the first place – and a fatal split occurred between the king and his chief allies, Gerard de Ridefort and Reginald of Chatillon on the one side, and the former regent, Raymond of Tripoli, on the other.

Reginald was, if anything, even more unpopular than Guy, and with good reason. After committing atrocities in Cyprus, then under Byzantine control, Reginald mounted an expedition to relieve Syrian Christians of their cattle. On his way back to Antioch, he was captured by Muslim forces and ransomed. No one came forward to pay up, and Reginald remained incarcerated for the next 16 years. After being released around 1176, Reginald participated – bravely, by some accounts – in the campaigns against Saladin, but he remained the Franks' loose cannon. In 1182, he had caused the maximum possible outrage in the Arab world when he had embarked upon a series of raids into Muslim territory from the Red Sea, attacking merchant ships and pilgrims on the way to Mecca; not satisfied with this, a splinter group made for Mecca, planning to dig up the body of the Prophet. Muslim forces under Saladin's brother Malik intercepted them before they reached the Holy City and wasted no time in executing them. With Guy's accession to the throne, however, Reginald was off again. Blithely disregarding Raymond's four-year truce with Saladin, Reginald attacked a large Muslim caravan; in the battle, all the caravan's Egyptian guards were slaughtered.

During late 1186 and early 1187 – around the same time that Reginald was running amok – the Templar Grand Master, Gerard de Ridefort, tried to persuade King Guy to heal the rift between himself and Raymond of Tripoli. Raymond, like Reginald, had spent time in Muslim jails, but, unlike him, had undertaken the study of Arabic and had developed an interest in Muslim culture. It was this Muslim-friendly position – adopted by the Templars themselves at other times under less maniacal Grand Masters than Gerard – that led Raymond to approach Saladin and negotiate a truce that would leave Tripoli and Galilee free from Muslim aggression whilst Raymond dealt with the ever-worsening situation with his co-religionists to the south.

The two sides agreed to attempt to broker a deal at Tiberias, which was in Raymond's territory, on the shores of the Sea of Galilee. Whilst Gerard and a Templar contingent – together with Roger des Moulins and a force of Hospitaller knights – were staying at the Templar castle of Le Fève, en route for Tiberias, Raymond sent word that he had allowed a Muslim scouting party into the area, on condition that they kept the peace. This was the red rag to Gerard's bull, and he immediately ordered an attack on the Muslims. A day or so later, on 1 May 1187, the Frankish troops encountered Saladin's men at the Springs of Cresson, north of Nazareth. Despite the fact that the Christian forces only numbered 90 Templars, with another 50 secular knights, against a Muslim strength of 7,000, Gerard ordered an attack. The Marshal of the Temple, James of Mailly, and the Master of the Hospital, Roger des Moulins, both urged retreat, but Gerard accused them of cowardice. James of Mailly is said to have replied, 'I shall die in battle a brave man, it is you who will flee as a traitor.'[15] The Marshal's words proved to be prophetic: in the bloodbath that followed, the Christian forces were almost completely wiped out; only Gerard and two other Templars escaped with their lives.

If precipitating one military disaster was not enough, Gerard was to reprise his role as the military adviser to whose advice one should do the exact opposite a matter of weeks later. As Saladin moved inexorably south towards Jerusalem, he took the city of Tiberias, trapping Raymond of Tripoli's wife within its walls. The Franks held a council of war at Acre on 1 July.

Raymond, whose rift with King Guy was now healed, advised staying put, despite the fact that his wife was held by the enemy, as Saladin's army was too big to engage successfully. The king seemed to be in agreement until, later that night, Gerard advised an attack, convincing the king that it would be shameful to sacrifice Tiberias. Whether Gerard's advice was due to a near-suicidal streak in the Grand Master, or whether it was because he hated Raymond and couldn't bear the thought of agreeing to anything the Count of Tripoli suggested, he managed to change the king's mind.

The crusader army marched north at dawn, until it reached the village of Lubiya. They were constantly harried by Muslim archers, and were suffering greatly from thirst. The Templars, who formed the rearguard, asked if they could stop for the night. Whether the request came directly from Gerard it is not known, but King Guy agreed. Raymond, who was leading the vanguard, is alleged to have said when he heard this, 'Lord God, the war is over. We are dead men. The kingdom is finished.' The army was camped on an arid hill known as the Horns of Hattin and they had no water; the well was dry. During the night, Saladin's men set fire to the scrub at the foot of the hill, and the breeze carried it upwards, choking the Franks. At dawn on 4 July, Saladin's forces attacked. Crippled by the summer heat, thirst and smoke, the crusader army stood no chance. It was a disaster greater even than Cresson.

Muslim custom decrees that a man who is offered food or water shall be spared. After his capture, Saladin offered a glass of water to King Guy, who gratefully accepted it. The glass was not offered to Reginald of Chatillon, the most hated man in the whole of the East; instead, Reginald was offered the choice of conversion or death, and he refused to convert. Saladin wasted no more time and personally decapitated him. The Templar and

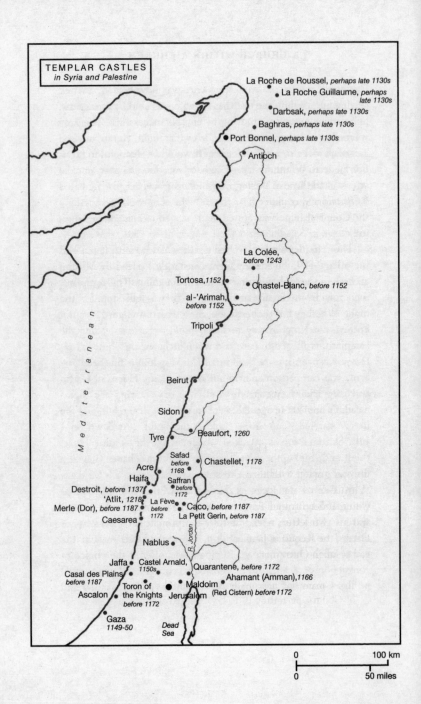

TEMPLAR CASTLES
in Syria and Palestine

La Roche de Roussel, *perhaps late 1130s*
La Roche Guillaume, *perhaps late 1130s*
Darbsak, *perhaps late 1130s*
Baghras, *perhaps late 1130s*
Port Bonnel, *perhaps late 1130s*
Antioch

La Colée, *before 1243*
Tortosa, *1152*
Chastel-Blanc, *before 1152*
al-'Arimah, *before 1152*
Tripoli

Beirut

Sidon

Tyre
Beaufort, *1260*

Safad *before 1168*
Chastellet, *1178*
Acre
Haifa
Destroit, *before 1137*
Saffran *before 1172*
'Atlit, *1218*
La Fève *before 1172*
Merle (Dor), *before 1187*
Caco, *before 1187*
La Petit Gerin, *before 1187*
Caesarea

Nablus

Jaffa
Castel Arnald, *1150s*
Quarantene, *before 1172*
Casal des Plains *before 1187*
Ahamant (Amman), *1166*
Toron of the Knights *before 1172*
Maldoim (Red Cistern) *before 1172*
Ascalon
Jerusalem

Gaza *1149-50*

R. Jordan
Dead Sea

Mediterranean

0   100 km
0   50 miles

Hospitaller captives were given the same ultimatum – apostasy or death. Saladin's hatred of the military orders was founded upon his belief that they were the most fanatical of the Frankish warriors, and the aftermath of Hattin proved him right. The Templars were so eager for martyrdom that there was almost a stampede to be the first to be beheaded. All 230 Templar prisoners – and those of the Hospital – were executed. Only Gerard de Ridefort was spared.

After Hattin, it was only a matter of time before Jerusalem itself was in Saladin's hands. The week after Hattin, Acre fell, followed in September by Ascalon and Gaza. Finally, on 2 October 1187, Saladin entered Jerusalem. He allowed the Church of the Holy Sepulchre to remain in Christian hands, but the cross from the Dome of the Rock was taken down and dragged through the streets where it was trampled upon and beaten with sticks. Although a small contingent of non-military Hospitallers were allowed to remain for a limited time in the Hospital to continue the work they had originally been founded for – the care of sick pilgrims – the Templars were forced to surrender their headquarters at the al-Aqsa mosque. They would never set foot there again.

The Third Crusade

Europe reacted with horror to the news that Jerusalem was lost. With Gerard de Ridefort in captivity, the Templar Grand Commander Brother Terence assumed leadership of the Order, and his two letters – the first written a matter of weeks after Hattin, the second in January 1188 – described the disasters that had befallen Outremer:

> 'How many and how great the calamities with which the anger of God has permitted us to be scourged at this present time, as

a consequence of our sins, we can explain neither by letters nor by tearful voice.'[16]

He goes on to write about Hattin and the loss of Acre, saying that Christian forces cannot hold out much longer 'unless we immediately receive divine aid and your [i.e. Western] help' as the infidel are 'cover[ing] the entire face of the land... like ants'.[17]

The letter was nominally addressed to Pope Urban III and to Philip of Alsace, Count of Flanders, the only major European leader who had visited the East that decade, but was also intended to be circulated as widely as possible. It reached Urban at Verona, delivered by Templar couriers, and it had a devastating effect; so much so that it probably hastened Urban's end. His successor, Gregory VIII, was already ancient and only reigned for two months, yet in that time, he called for the kings of Europe to cease fighting one another for seven years and devote themselves instead to freeing the East from the oppression of the infidel. King William II of Sicily, who, when he first heard the news, replaced his regal attire with sackcloth and went into retreat, at once sent a fleet of galleys to relieve Antioch. Something akin to the righteous furore surrounding the First Crusade began to sweep through Europe, with the Crusade being seen as a rite of passage, where one was not so much participating in order to gain absolution – as had been the case with the First Crusade – but in order to vanquish evil and prove one's courage in the field. This romanticisation reached its apogee in the monk Peter of Blois' *Passio Reginaldi*, in which the recently deceased Reginald of Chatillon is portrayed not as the murdering maniac that he was, but as a saint and martyr.

As preparations got under way in Europe for a new crusade, the Templars were at the forefront of the campaign to keep the remaining Christian possessions in the East out of Saladin's control. After the loss of Jerusalem, a fierce Christian counter-attack kept Tyre in crusader hands. Several Templar castles fell, principally Safad north-west of the Sea of Galilee and Gaston, which may have been the first castle the Order took over in the Amanus March in the 1130s. The other main military order, the Hospitallers, lost Belvoir, Kerak and Montréal. But significant possessions remained – Antioch, Tyre and Tripoli all held out against Muslim forces. Both King Guy and Gerard de Ridefort were released by Saladin, and re-entered the fray.

Despite the gravity of the situation facing the Franks, the old factional disputes were still alive, as Guy found out when he attempted to re-enter Tyre. That the city held out against Saladin was largely due to the unexpected arrival of a fleet under the German prince, Conrad of Montferrat, who duly put himself in charge of the city after Saladin gave up attempting to take it in early 1188. In Conrad's eyes, the disasters of the previous year meant that Guy was no longer king. Guy's next move was against Acre, where he attempted to besiege the city in the autumn of 1189. That he was attempting to take a city at all suggests that Gerard de Ridefort had been advising him, and a contingent of Templars were among the forces that assembled around Acre. This time, Gerard's luck ran out, and he died fighting outside the walls of Acre on 4 October. When Acre was finally retaken, on 12 July 1191, the Templars had a new Grand Master and the *Reconquista* against Saladin, under the King of England, Richard the Lionheart, was finally under way.

The Third Crusade marks perhaps the highpoint between the Templars and a crusade leader. Although during the Second Crusade, the Templars had proved themselves indispensable, this was at least due in part to their financial commitment to it, and it was only with the Third Crusade that they really came into their own as a fighting force. This was in large part due to the new Grand Master, Robert de Sablé, who was a vassal and trusted friend of Richard the Lionheart. Richard, although notorious as England's absent king – he was only in the country for six months of his ten-year reign – was a brilliant military commander, ably supported by the cautious Robert. Within two months of Acre, Richard's tactical skill would show its hand.

On 7 September 1191 Saladin attacked the crusader army as it marched south from Caesarea, just outside the forest of Arsuf. During the march, the Templars had formed the rearguard, while the Hospitallers complemented them at the front of the column. During the battle itself, Richard reversed the roles of the orders to great effect, knowing that he could rely on their discipline in the field. Although Muslim losses were light, it was Saladin's first defeat since the victory at Hattin, and it marked a turning point for the Crusade. It brought renewed hope to the coastal cities still under Christian control that Jerusalem itself could be retaken.

The Third Crusade, however, was not to retake the Holy City. Although Richard came within sight of its walls, both Robert de Sablé and the Hospitaller Grand Master Geoffroi de Donjon urged caution, pointing out that even if Jerusalem could be taken, retaining it after the departure of the crusaders would be difficult, if not impossible. Richard agreed with the Grand Masters, and decided his next course of action would be to refortify Ascalon.

Richard was keen to return to England, to deal with his increasingly troublesome brother John. His main priority before he left, therefore, was to ensure that the succession issue was decided. His own favoured candidate was Guy of Lusignan, but he was outvoted by the kingdom's barons, who wanted Conrad of Montferrat to be the next King of Jerusalem instead. Conrad, however, was murdered by the Assassins in the streets of Acre, leaving the way open for Richard's nephew, Henry of Champagne, to succeed. (Some have suspected Richard of ordering Conrad's death, but this is disputed.) This left the former king, Guy of Lusignan, to be dealt with, and it was decided that he should be given Cyprus, an island that had been a thorn in the sides of both Richard and the Templars.

When Richard was en route to Outremer in early 1191, two of his ships had ended up on Cyprus. The island was then under the control of Isaac Ducas Comnenus, a particularly slippery Byzantine prince who had just made a pact with Saladin. The first of Richard's ships had contained crusaders, while the second carried Richard's betrothed, Berengaria of Navarre, and her chaperone, his sister Joan, the Dowager Queen of Sicily. Richard arrived a week later and demanded the release of the prisoners. Isaac refused, and Richard, perhaps seeing Cyprus as a source of useful booty for the Third Crusade, launched an attack against Isaac's forces. The Byzantine, hated by the islanders, was quickly overpowered and a Western garrison was installed on the island. After Richard had left for the Holy Land, word reached him that the local population was proving difficult to control, and the new Templar Grand Master, Robert de Sablé – who was almost certainly elected to the position at Richard's behest – offered to buy the island from Richard for 100,000 *besants*. Richard agreed, and a Templar garrison left for the island. However, they too had trouble with the locals, culminating in their fort at Nicosia being besieged on 4 April 1192, and realised that, without a larger garrison, holding the island would be a thankless task. They therefore sold it back to Richard. Richard felt that this would be the ideal place to put the habitually ineffectual Guy, and sold the island to him for 60,000 *besants*, making the former king now Guy of Cyprus in the process.

Saladin proved to be less easy to dispose of, and negotiations dragged on. In an attempt to force him to come to terms, the Franks successfully attacked the castle of Daron, which lay to the south of Ascalon. Richard returned to Acre just as Saladin made a surprise move against Jaffa, taking the town after three days. Richard, accompanied by only 80 knights – Templars amongst them – 400 archers and 2,000 Italian mercenaries, improvised a counterattack and beat off the much larger Muslim force. Negotiations were concluded not long after. Richard agreed to demolish Ascalon, while Saladin agreed to recognise Christian possessions along the coast. Furthermore, Christians and Muslims were to be allowed to cross each other's territory, and Christian pilgrims were free to visit Jerusalem and the Holy Places.

On 9 October 1192, Richard left the Holy Land with a Templar escort. He never returned. Saladin died the following year. A tenuous peace descended on the land beyond the sea.

The Templars at the turn of the Thirteenth Century

The Templars, like much of the Latin East after the Third Crusade, found themselves trying to rebuild the hold they had had before the disasters of the late 1180s. Despite the fact that Christian pilgrims were allowed into Jerusalem, they themselves were not, and so they established new headquarters at Acre, which now became the most important city in the Latin East, and the Templars' base for the next 100 years. The Order had had a presence in the city for decades, and the German monk Theoderich saw it in the 1170s. The chronicler known as the Templar of Tyre, writing in the mid-thirteenth century, described it as:

'The strongest place of the city, largely situated along the seashore, like a castle. At its entrance it had a high and strong tower, the wall of which was 28 feet thick. On each side of the tower was a smaller tower, and on each of these was a gilded lion passant, as large as an ox. These four lions [together with] the gold and the labour, cost 1,500 Saracen *besants*, and were noble to look upon. On the other side, near the Street of the Pisans, there was another tower, and near this tower on the Street of St Anne, was a large and noble palace, which was the Master's. In front of the house of the nuns of St Anne was another high tower, which had bells, and a very noble and high church. There was another ancient tower on the seashore, which Saladin had built 100 years before, in which the Temple kept its treasure, and it was so close to the sea that the waves washed against it. Within the Temple area there were other beautiful and noble houses, which I will not describe here.'[18]

Although Acre, long familiar to the Order, proved to be a sound choice of location for their new base of operations, it was the Templars' attempts to re-establish themselves in the Amanus March, which had been amongst their very first fortified possessions in the East, that illustrate how much damage had been done by Saladin's campaigns.

The Templar castles Gaston (Baghras) and Darbsaq had both fallen to Saladin's forces during September 1188, severely weakening the Order's powerbase in the region. Gaston proved to be a drain on resources, however, and, in 1191, the Muslims abandoned it. Prince Leo of Cilician Armenia then occupied and refortified it. When the Templars attempted to gain access to the fortress, they were refused, and so began a long campaign to wrest control of it from Leo. The situation was made infinitely more complicated by Leo's war with Antioch, the precarious position of the Armenian Church and the rival claims made by

Leo's descendants and those of his Antiochene rival, Bohemond III. An intermittent campaign was conducted between the Templars and Leo's forces until 1211, when, in a series of attacks on the Templars and their holdings, the recently elected Grand Master, Guillaume de Chartres, was wounded and Pope Innocent III subsequently excommunicated Leo. The Armenian Church had only been reconciled with Rome since 1197, and Leo evidently felt that his excommunication put him politically beyond the pale, so he restored Gaston and other Templar holdings to the Order between 1213 and 1216.

The sense of the Order – and Christendom – re-establishing itself after the end of the Third Crusade is also evident in the actions of Pope Innocent III (1198–1216). In 1199, he wrote to the leaders of Outremer complaining that no one seemed to have the heart for a new crusade (which he himself was very keen to promote). He also published a series of bulls that reiterated the Templars' special status, and demanded that the clergy respect the Order's rights and privileges. He reminded the clergy in no uncertain terms that the Templars had a right to their own burial grounds and had the freedom to erect churches on their own land and warned them against doing violence to any serving brother or to Templar property. Furthermore, the clergy were asked not to forget that the Templars were exempt from paying tithes, that they should be left in peace to collect those tithes due to them from their own lands, and that the clergy were expressly forbidden to divert any of these funds their way; the clergy were also not to excommunicate Templar churches and those who broke into Templar houses were to be punished; the clergy were to prevent brothers who were serving in the Order for a set period of time from leaving early; bishops who forced Templars to fight other Christians (as happened in parts of the Iberian peninsula and eastern Europe) were condemned; and the clergy were instructed to protect the property and privileges of the Templars against usurpers, and were to excommunicate those who disobeyed. Just in case the clergy did not get the point, Innocent also reissued the bull that had given the Templars their privileges in the first place, *Omne datum optimum*.

Innocent also directly addressed the Order, warning its members not to abuse any of their privileges, knowing full well that they were often accused of the sin of pride. He complained that they gave full Christian burial to anybody, as long as they had some money to pay for it, not bothering to find out whether they had been excommunicated or had some other reason for not being allowed to be laid to rest in consecrated ground. In prophetic words, Innocent warned the Order that if they did not change their ways, they would become agents of the Devil.

The Other Military Orders

One unexpected development in the Latin East after the end of the Third Crusade was the establishment of a new military order. In 1197, German crusaders had arrived in the East; they were largely unsuccessful, their sole military contribution being their participation in the capture of Beirut that year. Most of the German crusaders returned home, but a number of knights remained in the East, and joined a field hospital that had been set up in 1190 by merchants from Bremen and Lübeck. During the siege of Acre in 1191 they were said to have welcomed brothers from the Hospital of St Mary of the Germans, which, tradition holds, was founded in Jerusalem in 1127. The new hospital's first base in Acre was a tent on the shore made from a ship's mainsail. When the knights joined, they became the Teutonic Knights of St Mary's Hospital of Jerusalem, and on 5 March 1198, the

Teutonic Knights were accepted as an order of the church at the Temple compound in Acre.

The Teutonic Knights were the last of the three great military orders to be founded. The first of them, the Hospitallers, had been founded before the formation of the Templars, sometime around 1070. The Hospital – founded by a group of merchants from Amalfi – was originally that of St John the Almoner, and it operated an infirmary and guest house for pilgrims near the Church of Holy Sepulchre. The first Grand Master was Peter Gerard, who was elected in about 1100. As soon as the Kingdom of Jerusalem was established, Godfroi de Bouillon donated lands to the Order, and many others followed suit, with the result that the Hospitallers had extensive holdings in Europe as well as the East. The capture of Jerusalem in 1099 led naturally to the influx of a greater number of pilgrims than ever, and it was decided that a more prominent patron saint should be adopted for the Order: John the Almoner was replaced by John the Baptist. The Hospital was recognised as an order by Pope Paschal II (1099–1118) in 1113.

The Order's second Grand Master, Raymond de Puy, oversaw the Hospital's adoption of an increasingly military role. In the early years, it is possible that Templars were used to guard the Hospital's establishments, but during the 1120s it seems that the Hospitallers themselves started to militarise. A Hospitaller constable is mentioned in documents dating from 1126,[19] but the first firm date for military activity is 1136, when King Fulk gave the Order the castle of Gibelin, on the Gaza–Hebron road. Like the Templars, the Hospitallers received papal privileges: Innocent II (1130–43) forbade bishops to interdict Hospitaller chapels; Anastasius IV (1153–54) gave them their own priests; while Adrian IV (1154–59) gave them their own churches. Their rule evolved slowly, with Raymond being guided by pragmatic concerns. Like the Teutonic Knights after them, some of the Hospital's statutes were modelled on those of the Templars.

In addition to the Hospital and the Teutonic Knights, there were several smaller orders active in the East. The Hospital of St Lazarus was the third military order to be founded after the Temple and the Hospital of St John. Originating probably from a Greek or Armenian leper house in Jerusalem, the Order was set up solely for knights who had contracted leprosy. It was taken over by the Hospital of St John during the early 1100s, and it is said that the first Hospitaller Grand Master, Peter Gerard, also acted as the Grand Master of St Lazarus. According to legend, all their subsequent Grand Masters were lepers. They established a chain of houses for lepers across the East and Europe, which became known as 'Lazar Houses', and were chiefly known for their hospitaller work, although they participated in a number of engagements in the East alongside the Templars and Hospitallers. The Templar Rule demanded that a brother who caught leprosy must transfer to the Order of St Lazarus.[20]

The Knights of Our Lady of Montjoie were recognised as an order by a bull issued by Pope Alexander III (1159–81) in 1180. The Order was founded by a Spanish knight, Count Rodrigo, taking its name from the castle of Montjoie just outside of Jerusalem (the name itself deriving from the cries of joy that pilgrims were said to have uttered upon first seeing the Holy City). The Order – never numerous at the best of times – seemed to have had trouble gaining recruits, and, after the disasters of 1187, the surviving brothers retired to Aragon, where they changed their name to the Order of Trufac.

The Hospitallers of St Thomas of Canterbury, also known as the Knights of St Thomas Acon, were founded around the same time as the Teutonic Knights. Their origins were also from the time of the Third Crusade: William, the Dean of St Paul's, was so moved by the plight of the English crusaders that, after the capture of Acre in 1191, he bought a small chapel and cemetery. The hospital that he founded was restricted to Englishmen, although many preferred to join the Templars and the Hospitallers instead. Like their better-known contemporaries, they received donations of land in the East and in Europe. They are thought to have militarised around the time of the Fifth Crusade.

Military Tactics

The Templars' reputation in the field was unsurpassed. When the Franks were crushed at Hattin, Saladin ordered that all the captive Templars and Hospitallers be executed, such was his conviction that the military orders were the Franks' main weapon against Islam. (Indeed, Saladin viewed the two orders as 'impure races'.[21])

The Templars – as did the secular Franks – employed cavalry and infantry. The former comprised mounted knights and sergeants, the latter archers and troops armed with axes and spears. The knights were the mediaeval equivalent of a tank, with their great war horses often standing up to 17 hands high. The horses – known as *destriers* – were taught to kick, butt and bite. The sergeants were also mounted, but wore lighter armour and rode in the rear.

Tactics were simple, but, when timed properly, were devastatingly effective. Initially, the infantry would provide cover, before the cavalry charge, which would form the main attack. A properly timed charge would wipe out everything in its path; misjudged charges led to disasters such as the Springs of Cresson. During the melée, the Templars were sworn to stay in the field as long as the Order's distinctive black and white banner, known as the *beauseant*, remained aloft. As soon as the *beauseant* was lost to sight, the Templars would rally to the Hospitaller banner or, if that too was down, then any remaining Christian banner. Their vows meant that they were usually the first into the field, and the last to leave.

In the early years of the Latin East, the Templars quickly developed a fearsome reputation as the best-trained soldiers the Franks had, showing almost suicidal bravery at times. This reached an apogee during the Mastership of Gerard de Ridefort, who died during a reckless attack at Acre. However, as the twelfth century gave way to the thirteenth, the Templars began to retreat from their earlier zeal and grew ever more cautious in battle.

The Temple and the Empire

Innocent's plans for a new crusade in the East finally materialised in 1218, although he himself did not live to see it. After Innocent's death in July 1216, he was succeeded by Honorius III (1216–27), who was determined to get the crusading machinery in motion. Although the Templars had played little or no role in the Fourth Crusade (1202–04) – mainly due to the crusade's failure to actually make it to Palestine after sacking Constantinople – they were heavily involved in the Fifth from the outset.

A crusade fund was established at the Paris Temple, where the Templar treasurer, Brother Haimard, oversaw donations. Honorius wrote to the Templar Grand Master, Guillaume de Chartres, and also to his opposite number in the Hospital, Garin de Montaigu, ordering them to meet the crusade's leaders, King Andrew of Hungary and Leopold, Duke of Austria, on Cyprus. As things turned out, the two men and their respective armies arrived separately in the East in the autumn of 1217. Initial plans to attack Damascus were shelved after the somewhat lacklustre campaign of November 1217 in favour of mounting a campaign in Egypt, with the intention of capturing the key city of Damietta. With reinforcements under the King of Jerusalem, John of Brienne (1210–25), the crusaders – including contingents of Templars, Hospitallers and Teutonic Knights – landed at Damietta in June 1218. It was here that the Templar Grand Master, who had been unwell since the previous autumn, died, and was succeeded by Garin de Montaigu's brother, Peter. For the first and only time, the Orders of the Temple and the Hospital were under the control of the same family. (A third brother, Eustorge, was Archbishop of Nicosia.)

Damietta was swiftly captured. Oliver of Paderborn, the master of Cologne's cathedral school, who went on the Fifth Crusade, wrote in admiration of the Templars' ability to fight in the waterlogged terrain of the Nile Delta, using both a fleet of ships and pontoons, and being able to negotiate the swamps on horseback. Warfare of this sort would not normally be waged in the sun-baked hills and valleys of Palestine, and that the Templars were so effective in the capture of Damietta proved that they were military strategists and engineers of genius.

The crusaders' initial success moved the Egyptian Sultan, al-Kamil, Saladin's brother, to offer them Jerusalem in return for Damietta. Pelagius, the Papal legate and self-appointed leader of the Crusade, rejected the offer. As with Richard and the question of Jerusalem on the Third Crusade, the Montaigu brothers had argued that Jerusalem could not be held unless the lands beyond the Jordan were also ceded to the crusaders, and this was something that was not part of al-Kamil's offer. They decided to wait for further reinforcements before continuing with the Crusade, believing that the cause would be greatly aided by the arrival of the Holy Roman Emperor, Frederick II. When it became apparent that an Imperial army was not going to materialise, Pelagius ordered an advance up the Nile. The Templars were reluctant, believing that the Crusade's resources were overstretched. Their misgivings proved to be correct. When the Frankish army reached the town of Mansurah, al-Kamil's forces cut off the crusaders' rear and blocked their path ahead by opening the sluice gates; the Crusade was literally flooded into submission. Pelagius had no choice but to accept al-Kamil's terms and surrender Damietta. A truce of eight years was also agreed.

Despite Frederick's failure to appear, the general feeling remained that he would fulfil his vow to go on crusade, a vow he had taken at his coronation in Frankfurt in 1212. The grandson of Frederick Barbarossa, who had died while on the Third Crusade in 1190, Frederick II was one of the most extraordinary characters of his age. He was raised in Sicily and was elected king at the age of three. He had a naturally enquiring mind, and became fluent in not just Italian, French and German, but also Greek, Latin and Arabic. In choosing to rule from Sicily, Frederick created a political and cultural gap that was far wider than the straits of Messina, which separated the island from the Italian mainland, might suggest: he had a pronounced interest in Arabic culture, and his bodyguard was made up entirely of Saracens. He was rumoured to be an atheist, and certainly had what might be termed a scientific outlook on nature, which led to a number of bizarre and sometimes cruel experiments: children were raised in complete silence in order to observe what language they would utter when they were old enough to talk (this would therefore prove what language Adam and Eve had spoken in the Garden of Eden[22]); a man was imprisoned in a wine barrel to see if his soul could be seen departing from his body at the moment of death; two men – one indolent, the other active – were killed and then dissected in order to find out how their lifestyles had affected their internal organs. Rumours abounded about Frederick's private life, and he certainly seems to have had somewhat liberal attitudes to sex. He defended the Jews of Germany against charges of the ritual murder of Christian children, and, at one point, is said to have seriously considered converting to Islam, which would have made him, as Holy Roman Emperor, neither holy, Roman nor emperor.

Frederick and his army finally landed at Acre on 7 September 1228. It had been a difficult passage: Frederick's forces had to put in at Otranto because of illness; and this delay had enraged the new pope, Gregory IX, so much that he excommunicated the Emperor. When he finally set sail again the following spring, Frederick was excommunicated again for attempting to go on crusade while excommunicated. Frederick was not unduly bothered by this, but, by the time he reached Acre that autumn, word of his excommunications had spread among the clergy and baronage of Outremer. This officially meant that Frederick could no longer command the Crusade, and the Latins were split along Papal–Imperial lines. Most of the Frankish barons, the Templars and the Hospitallers sided with the Pope – the Templars, after all, were answerable to none save the pontiff himself – while the Teutonic Knights sided with Frederick. Furthermore, Frederick's wife, Isabel, had died giving birth to their son Conrad that May, and, as his claim to the crown of Jerusalem was through his marriage to her, he was technically no longer king either, merely the regent for the infant Conrad.

Perhaps because of his dubious status as both leader of the Sixth Crusade and as King of Jerusalem, Frederick began to assert his authority by marching to 'Atlit and demanding that the Templars hand the castle over to a German garrison (presumably to be placed under the control of the Teutonic Knights). The Templars refused to let Frederick in and he returned to Acre. His next move was to march on Jaffa. The Templars and the Hospitallers would not accept Frederick's command, and followed the Imperial forces a day's journey behind. By the time they had reached Arsuf, Frederick delegated his command to his generals, therefore making it possible for the two main military orders to rejoin the Crusade. Now expecting to engage the enemy, the Templars were to be frustrated by a coup of staggering proportions – Frederick regained Jerusalem through diplomacy.

The recovery of the Holy City came as a complete surprise to the military orders and to the barons of Outremer; to Frederick, however, it was something he had possibly been expecting. Even before he left Sicily, Frederick had received the Emir Fakhr ad-Din ibn as-Shaikh, al-Kamil's ambassador, at court in Palermo; the Emir brought the Emperor news that al-Kamil would return Jerusalem to Christian control if Frederick promised to help the Sultan in his campaign to recapture Damascus. Frederick had not given al-Kamil a definite answer, and, during the negotiations conducted while on crusade, the subject had naturally come up again. By this time, however, Frederick had received news that the situation back home had taken a severe turn for the worse, with war breaking out between an Imperial army under Reginald of Spoleto, and a papal army under the former King of Jerusalem, John of Brienne, and he was anxious to return to Palermo. Although the thought of a successful Christian–Muslim alliance against al-Kamil's enemies in Damascus might have appealed to Frederick's ego, it would have been the greatest outrage of all time in the eyes of the Pope and Western leaders; quite what would have happened is difficult to imagine. A compromise was therefore reached in which Frederick and al-Kamil saved face – Jerusalem was returned to the Franks, but the Temple Mount was to remain in Muslim control. The city itself was to remain undefended, being connected to the coastal cities by a thin corridor of land. The military orders were forbidden from carrying out reinforcements on their castles, and a ten-year truce between the two leaders was agreed.

Despite this historic achievement, the recovery of Jerusalem led to the pious on both sides of accusing their respective leaders of treachery, and it very nearly led to a civil war among the Franks. Frederick was crowned King of Jerusalem in the Church of the Holy Sepulchre on 17 March 1229, despite the fact that the city had been placed under interdict by the Patriarch of Jerusalem, Gerold of Lausanne, should the Emperor arrive. The interdict forbade any church ceremonies from taking place whilst Frederick was within the walls of the city, but it made no difference – with no priests to crown him, Frederick simply crowned himself. The Templars and the Hospitallers stayed away, leaving only the loyal Teutonic Knights to guard the Emperor and King. Their great Grand Master, Herman von Salza, delivered an oration in which Frederick forgave the Pope for opposing him (a none too subtle reference to Frederick's double excommunication), and promised to do everything he could to defend the Church and the Empire. Frederick signed himself God's 'Vicar on Earth', a title which was normally reserved for the pontiff, thus throwing down the gauntlet. For Frederick, the enemy was not al-Kamil, but the Papacy.

After the ceremony, Frederick made a tour of Jerusalem. With typical Muslim diplomacy, al-Kamil had ordered the *muezzins* not to call the faithful to prayer while Frederick was in the city. Frederick, however, apparently wanted to hear the prayer-call – citing it as his reason for coming to Jerusalem – and when he entered the Dome of the Rock, he threw out a priest who had attempted to enter with the Imperial entourage, threatening to pluck out the man's eyes if he attempted it again.

Frederick then noticed a wooden lattice that had been placed over a window inside the Dome. It was explained to him that it had been placed there to keep the sparrows out, and Frederick, using the disparaging Muslim term for the Franks, replied, 'God has now sent you pigs.'

It was when Frederick returned to Acre that the 'pigs' nearly rose against him. He found Gerold and the Templars assembling forces to wrest Jerusalem from his control and attack Damascus. A tense stand-off ensued outside the city walls. It descended into a slanging match, with Frederick hurling insults at both the Patriarch and the Templars, in particular the Grand Master, Peter de Montaigu. Things had reached a spectacular all-time low in Templar–Imperial relations, so much so that both the Grand Master and the Emperor were each concerned for their physical safety. According to the chronicler Philip of Novara, Frederick was planning to kidnap a number of Frankish barons – and Peter de Montaigu – and have them tried at a kangaroo court before having them executed. Counter-propaganda circulated that the Templars were planning to assassinate Frederick whilst he was in Jerusalem, and the Emperor, possibly aware of the plot, only spent two nights in the city. Before Frederick left the Holy Land, he attempted to storm the Temple compound in Acre without success. When he finally did leave, at dawn on 1 May 1229, the jeering crowds pelted him with dung.

Frederick's return to the West did not mark the end of his involvement in the affairs of Outremer. In 1231, his *bailli*, or representative, Richard Filangieri, arrived with an Imperial force and tried to seize Acre. Although unsuccessful, he did manage to establish a base at Tyre, where he remained a thorn in the side of the Templars and the anti-Frederick camp. In 1232, the new Templar Grand Master, Armand de Périgord, was one of those who attempted to mediate between Filangieri and aggrieved

Frankish barons, but the attempt at reconciliation failed.

For the remainder of the 1230s, the Templars found themselves mainly concerned with local disputes, such as mounting
campaigns against local warlords like the Sultan of Hamah when
he failed to pay his annual tribute (protection money, in modern
parlance), or Muslim foragers who came too close to the
Templar stronghold of 'Atlit. It was only the imminent ending of
the ten-year truce between Frederick and al-Kamil that brought
the Templars back into the wider sphere, and saw them once
again adopt an anti-Imperial stance.

As 1239 approached, Pope Gregory preached a new crusade,
knowing how vulnerable Jerusalem was and fearful that Latin
possessions could be wiped off the map altogether. Only one
minor French noble, Theobald, Count of Champagne, took the
Cross. He arrived in the East on 1 September 1239 and, like the
participants of the Second Crusade before him, immediately
failed to grasp the complexities of the political situation in
Outremer. He found that the Franks, encouraged by the
Templars, had made an alliance with the ruler of Damascus – in
return for helping the Damascene forces against the Egyptians,
various lands seized by the Muslims would be returned to
Christian control. (This included the great Templar fortress of
Safad, which had been lost at Hattin, and the Order immediately
began restoring it to its former strength.) Theobald was
evidently unaware that al-Kamil had died in March of the previous year, resulting in anarchy in the Muslim world as his heirs
and claimants fought amongst themselves for al-Kamil's title. A
breakaway force under Henry, Count of Bar, decided to take
advantage of the situation by attacking Egypt; they were deci-
mated at Gaza. The blame fell not on Henry for underestimating
the size of the Egyptian army, but on the Templars and
Hospitallers – who had correctly assessed the danger posed by

the Egyptian forces – for refusing to support him.

Another crusade arrived the following year, under the leadership of Richard, Duke of Cornwall. Richard, nephew of the Lionheart, brother of Henry III of England and brother-in-law of the Emperor, clearly hoped to make an impact, and immediately set to work trying to free Christian prisoners from both Damascus and Cairo and to get the lands recently ceded to the Franks officially recognised by all parties. Richard's success was not to last. As soon as he had sailed for England, the Templars – unimpressed by Richard's efforts and suspicious of Egyptian duplicity – attacked the city of Hebron, then under Egyptian control, followed by the recapture of Nablus.

With Richard gone, the Templars found themselves in open conflict, not just with Imperial forces under Frederick's *bailli*, Richard Filangieri, but also with the Hospitallers. Although rivalry between the two Orders had always existed, settlements were usually found before any serious damage could be mutually inflicted. This time, however, the Hospital had opposed the Templars' attack on Hebron and Nablus, favouring, like Richard of Cornwall, diplomacy with the Egyptians. With the Duke of Cornwall safely bound for home, Filangieri tried to capture Acre, using the Hospital compound there as his base. The Templars, once more adopting the militant anti-Imperialist stance they had taken under Peter de Montaigu, responded by participating in the subsequent attack on the Hospitaller headquarters, besieging it for six months. The situation came to a head with the arrival in the East of Thomas of Aquino, the Count of Acerra, to accept the crown of Jerusalem on behalf of Frederick's son Conrad, who had now come of age. The Templar Grand Master, Armand de Périgord, was one of those who strongly opposed Conrad's accession, and instead lent support to Alice, Dowager Queen of Cyprus, on the grounds that she was the nearest heir and was therefore the only legitimate candidate for the Regency of Jerusalem. Genoese and Venetian forces arrived and, in the summer of 1243, they helped the Franks in evicting Filangieri, Count Thomas and all the rest of the Imperial party from Tyre, claiming – with dubious legality – that Conrad's claim to the throne of Jerusalem was invalid as he had not appeared in person to claim the crown.

The Franks had no time to put their house in order before a new crisis loomed, when, in early 1244, war broke out once again between Egypt and Damascus. This time, Egyptian forces were bolstered by the Khorezmian Turks, a tribe of ferocious nomads of mercenary persuasion. They flooded south from their base in Edessa and, on 11 July, attacked Jerusalem. The city finally fell a month later, on 23 August. The bones of Godfroi de Bouillon and other Kings of Jerusalem were disinterred and the Church of the Holy Sepulchre was set alight. Jerusalem would never again be under Christian control. But worse was to follow.

The Khorezmians headed south, joining forces with the Egyptian army at Gaza. On 17 October at La Forbie, the Frankish forces attacked the combined Muslim forces. It was a disaster; the Damascenes deserted and the remaining Christian forces were slaughtered, with at least 800 being taken prisoner and sold into slavery in Egypt. Among them was the Templar Grand Master, Armand de Périgord, who disappeared into the bowels of an Egyptian jail and was never seen again. The Order also lost somewhere between 260 and 300 knights; only 33 Templars, 26 Hospitallers and three Teutonic Knights returned from the field. The following year, Damascus fell to the Egyptians, and it seemed that Outremer's final hour had come.

The Fall of Acre

La Forbie was a disaster almost on par with Hattin. The West was shocked, and the possibility of a new crusade was considered. The only monarch who actually arrived in the East was Louis IX, the saintly French king, who had nearly died of fever around the same time that the Franks were being cut down on the field of La Forbie. His recovery, and the news that the East was once again in dire peril, decided the matter for him. After extensive preparations, he sailed from Aigues-Mortes in the Camargue on 25 August 1248, arriving on Cyprus on 17 September. Among the welcoming party was the new Templar Grand Master, Guillaume de Sonnac, who had been elected after the Order's failure to secure the release of Armand de Périgord from captivity in Egypt.[23]

The crusaders landed in Egypt on 5 June 1249, and found to their surprise that Damietta had been evacuated. They managed to take the city the following day, with the loss of only one life. Louis decided to march south towards Cairo, using the Templars to form the vanguard. Things seemed to be going the way of the Franks, a feeling reinforced when, on 23 November, the Egyptian Sultan, al-Sālih Aiyūb, died. However, they then spent a month trying to cross a branch of the Nile, but could not find a suitable place until a local Bedouin showed them the ford. On 8 February 1250, they began to cross, with the Templars and Richard, Count of Artois, Louis' brother, and William Longespée, the Earl of Salisbury, heading the column. It was at this point that things began to go badly wrong. On arriving on the opposite bank of the river, Richard decided to attack the Muslims rather than wait for the rest of the crusaders to finish crossing the river, and forced the Muslims to retreat to the nearby town of Mansurah. The Templars were angry at what they saw as Richard's arrogation of their role, and passed a message to the Count to that effect.

However, Foucaud du Merle, the knight who was holding the bridle of Richard's horse, was deaf, and failed to pass the message on. Richard charged off in pursuit of the Muslim forces and the Templars, now concerned at saving face, chased after him, determined to regain their position in the van. The Christian forces poured into Mansurah and found themselves trapped by wooden beams and other debris that had been used to close off the narrow streets. In the ensuing chaos, 300 knights died and 280 Templars; the instigator of the ill-fated attack, Richard of Artois, drowned under the weight of his armour while trying to swim to safety, while the Templar Grand Master Guillaume de Sonnac lost an eye. On 11 February, there was a second onslaught in which Guillaume lost his other eye and died later the same day. Although the Muslim forces were driven back, it became clear that taking Mansurah would not be easy.

Louis decided to sit it out, and waited. While the army was entrenched outside the walls of Mansurah, the Muslims had managed to cut the crusaders' supply lines from Damietta, depriving them of fresh food. To make matters worse, disease was spreading rapidly through the Frankish army. Louis suffered from acute dysentery and was continually visiting the latrine; indeed, so frequent were the king's visits that, according to the chronicler Joinville, his servants aided matters by cutting away the lower part of his drawers. Louis realised that he would have to negotiate, but the offer was rejected. On 5 April, the Franks began to retreat. The Muslims came after them and the casualties on the Christian side ran to several thousand. Only 14 survived from the military orders, including three Templars. As a final humiliation, most of the army – including Louis himself – was captured. Damietta was to be handed over in return for the king's life; the rest of the captives were to be ransomed for half a million *livres*.

Damietta was returned to Muslim control and, on 6 May, Louis was released. Before he left Egypt, there was still the matter of paying the rest of the ransom, and counting began on 7 May. By the end of the following day, it was apparent that they were still 30,000 *livres* short. Joinville suggested to the king that the amount be borrowed from the Templars, and Louis agreed. Joinville went to the Templars to ask for the money, but the Order's commander, Stephen of Otricourt, refused to hand the sum over on the grounds that he could only release the money to the people who had deposited it in the first place. Tempers began to fray and 'there were many hard and abusive words'[24] between Joinville and the Commander until the Templar Marshal, Reginald de Vichiers, suggested that, although they had sworn vows to protect their clients' money, there was nothing stopping Joinville from taking the money by force. Therefore, with the king's permission, Joinville went on board the Templar galley where the money was kept in the hold. However, the Templar treasurer refused to open the strongbox, perhaps owing to Joinville's somewhat haggard appearance after the deprivations of the retreat from Mansurah and also to the fact that he was wielding an axe. At this point, Reginald de Vichiers, clearly concerned that Joinville was about to commit an act of violence, intervened and ordered the treasurer to open the strongbox and hand the money over.

Louis arrived back in Acre on 13 May, and, with his support, Reginald de Vichiers was elected Grand Master of the Temple. This was partially to repay Reginald for his role in the king's release, but also for his involvement with the Crusade from its inception: as early as 1246, Reginald was acting on behalf of Louis in arranging shipping to carry the crusaders to the East. Louis stayed in Outremer for another four years, and he initially remained on close terms with the Templars. Indeed, when a son was born to Louis, the baby was delivered in the castle of 'Atlit, and Reginald acted as his godfather. Relations were soon strained, however, when Reginald attempted to form a new alliance with Damascus without consulting Louis. The king was furious, and made the Grand Master perform public penance for his insubordination.

Louis left the East in April 1254. Despite the failure in Egypt, the Crusade had achieved a number of things: fortifications were improved in key cities such as Caesarea, Jaffa, Sidon and Acre itself, and Louis pledged to assist in maintaining them by supplying a constant garrison of French troops. The inland castles – such as Safad – were all in the hands of the military orders, as they had proved too expensive for the secular baronage to run. Additionally, Louis had shown that Outremer could still be governed well provided that it had a single, strong leader behind whom the Frankish barons could unite. And in his six years in the East, he had injected a vast amount of money into the economy – 1.3 million *livres tournois*, about 11 or 12 times the annual income of his kingdom.[25]

When Louis left, he took his leadership and financial support with him. Unfortunately for the Franks, this coincided almost exactly with the rise of two new powers that would both threaten Outremer – the Mongols and the Mamluks. Of the two, the Mongols proved the most immediate threat. Indeed, such was the Frankish fear of them that it brought all three of the main military orders together. The Templars, Hospitallers and Teutonic Knights all agreed to put their habitual squabbles to one side in the name of defending Outremer (an achievement all the more impressive when one considers that civil war had broken out in the East shortly after Louis' departure, with the Templars and Teutonic Knights on one side, and the Hospitallers on the other). Letters were written and frantically dispatched to the

West. One Templar courier managed to make it to London in just 13 weeks, bearing a doom-laden account of the situation in the East, reminiscent of the letters of Brother Terence after the disasters of 1187:

> '... when they had read these letters, both the king [Henry III] and the Templars... gave way to lamentation and sadness, on a scale no one had ever seen before. For the news was that the Tartars [Mongols], advancing with an innumerable force, had already occupied and devastated the Holy Land almost up to Acre... unless help is quickly brought, a horrible annihilation will swiftly be visited upon the world.'[26]

On 3 September 1260, a horrible annihilation was indeed visited upon Outremer, but it was not the Franks who bore the brunt of it: it was the Mongols themselves. At 'Ain Jūlāt, south of Nazareth, a Mongol army was crushed by Mamluk forces under the sultan Saif-ad-Din Kutuz. The Mamluks, a caste of elite slave warriors who had been a permanent component of the Egyptian military for a century, had recently seized power in Egypt, bringing to an end the rule of Saladin's descendants. Kutuz himself was soon ousted, being assassinated the month following the victory at 'Ain Jūlāt. He was replaced as sultan by Baybars, who had fought in the Egyptian army at La Forbie and against Louis at Mansurah; he would do more damage to the Franks than any other Muslim leader since Saladin.

Baybars immediately set about destroying Frankish possessions in Outremer. The 1260s are a litany of Christian defeats, with even such great Templar castles as Safad and the Hospitaller stronghold of Krak des Chevaliers falling. The Pope, Clement IV, decided that a new crusade was called for, once the immediate problem of Sicily and Frederick's descendants had been dealt with. King Louis sent more money to the East via the Templars.

Templar Preceptories and Castles in the 12th Century

North Sea

Balantradoch

Clontarf

Willoughton

Temple Cowley   Temple Dinsley
Temple Guiting   Cressing
Templecombe   Shipley   London

Atlantic
Ocean

Sommereux
Laon
Beauvais
Paris   La Neuville
Orléans   Coulours

Nantes
Marmoutier

La Rochelle

Rodez   Richerenches
La Selve   Roaix
Saint-Gilles   Avignon   Albenga
Pézenas   Arles   Siena
Montsaunès   Douzens
Braga   Monzón   Mas-Deu   Rome
Chalamera   Grañera
Novillas   Palau
Ambel   Remolins   Barbara
Soure   Corbins
Tomar   Almourol
Santarém

Mediterranean Sea

| 0 | 250 km | 500 km |
| 0 | 150 miles | 300 miles |

No sooner had the funds been transferred, than further letters came from the East requesting more money to pay soldiers; appeals for help were unending. On 18 May 1268, Antioch fell and Thomas Bérard, the Templar Grand Master, decided that the Order's possessions in the Amanus March could no longer be successfully defended, and most were reluctantly abandoned. The seemingly unstoppable force of Baybars was only halted by the last crusade, that of Prince Edward of England, who persuaded the Mamluk sultan in April 1272 to agree to a ten-year truce. It was fortuitously timed. The Franks were in no position to hold out much longer, and Edward was forced to return to England upon the death of his father, Henry III, to assume the crown as Edward I.

At the Council of Lyons in May 1274, a new crusade was once again considered. Although the Templars played a promi-nent role in the talks – the Grand Master sat beside the Pope – an agreement could not be reached. Outremer was once again rent asunder by factional disputes, mainly centring around claims to the throne, with the Templars supporting Charles of Anjou, who had finally succeeded in wresting Sicily from the control of Frederick's son Conrad, whom he had had executed in Naples in 1268. Angry at what he saw as the Templars' adher-ence to no law save their own, the King of Jerusalem, Hugh III, simply upped and left for Cyprus, leaving no one in overall command. He tried to regain control of Outremer twice, in 1279 and 1283, but was unsuccessful on both occasions.

The Templars found themselves bogged down amid the various factions. They became involved in a civil war in the County of Tripoli between 1277 and 1282, an involvement that did nothing to enhance their reputation, and seems to have led to the Grand Master of the time, Guillaume de Beaujeu, as being widely regarded as untrustworthy. Guillaume did, however, get the Mamluks to agree to a new ten-year truce in 1282. In 1285, they broke it.

Baybars had died in July 1277, and his successor, Kalavun, was intent upon finishing the work that his predecessor had started. In April 1285, the coastal city of Latakia fell, followed by the Hospitaller fortress of al-Marqab the following month. The Templars were kept informed of Kalavun's plans by means of a double agent in the Mamluk hierarchy, and they were warned that Tripoli was in danger. Guillaume sent a messenger to warn the Tripolitans, but, perhaps because of the Grand Master's apparent political duplicity, the message was not believed. In desperation, a second messenger was despatched, also to no avail. Once the Tripolitans finally realised they were in danger, it was too late for reinforcements to reach them, and the city fell to Kalavun in April 1289.

Letters to the West continued at a frantic pace. Finally, in August 1290, a fresh wave of crusaders landed at Acre. Unfortunately, they were the sort of crusader who would not have looked out of place on the First Crusade – they were by and large buccaneers, criminals and drunkards who wasted no time in causing a riot in which many Muslim traders were killed. This was the pretext that Kalavun needed for an attack upon the city. Once more, the Templars had advance warning courtesy of their well-placed source close to Kalavun, but again, like the boy who cried wolf, Guillaume's warning was not believed.

On 5 April 1291, the Mamluks began their siege of Acre. Kalavun had died in November, but that had not stopped plans for an attack. His son, al-Ashraf Khalil, assumed command. Ten days later, Guillaume de Beaujeu led a daring night attack on al-Ashraf's forces, but the Templars were forced to retreat after becoming entangled in Mamluk tent ropes. On 15 May, a joint force of Templars and Hospitallers repelled a Mamluk assault on

St Anthony's Gate, but were not able to keep the Muslim forces out indefinitely, and on 18 May, they broke into Acre at the so-called 'Accursed Tower'. Guillaume de Beaujeu was apparently taking a well-deserved rest at the time, but, when he was told that the Mamluks were now inside the walls of the city, he rushed out into the mêlée without first stopping to put on all his armour. He was wounded in street fighting and died that evening. Within hours, the entire city apart from the Temple area was in Muslim hands and the harbour was full of ships taking refugees to Cyprus. On 25 May, the Templar Marshal, Peter de Sevrey, agreed to surrender if the Mamluks would guarantee the safety of all those who were taking refuge in the Temple compound. The Mamluks broke their word, but were beaten back by the Templars. There could now be no surrender. That night, the Templar Commander, Theobald Gaudin, sailed from Acre with the Templar treasure aboard his galley. Three days later, the Temple fell; everyone remaining inside fought to the death.

Theobald was elected Grand Master at Sidon by the remaining Templars there. A large Mamluk force appeared, and the Templars retreated to their stronghold. It was decided that Theobald would sail for Cyprus and bring back reinforcements. However, no reinforcements were forthcoming from Cyprus, only a message that it would be wise to leave the Holy Land; the Templars abandoned Sidon on 14 July. Haifa fell on the 30th, leaving only Tortosa and 'Atlit in Templar hands. They were effectively cut off, and had no choice but to evacuate: Tortosa was abandoned on 3 August, and the impregnable 'Atlit on 14 August. When the Mamluks reached 'Atlit, they dismantled it for fear that the Templars should return and reoccupy the one castle that had defeated even Baybars. But their fears proved unfounded. When Acre fell, Outremer had fallen with it. The Templars would never return to the Holy Land.

Fall and Trial
(1291–1314)

Theobald Gaudin did not long survive the loss of Acre. He died on 16 April, either in 1292 or 1293, and was succeeded by the man who – along with Hugues de Payen – is perhaps the best known Grand Master of the Order, Jacques de Molay. Jacques was probably around 50 years old when he was elected to the position, almost certainly in a Chapter Meeting at the Order's new headquarters at Limassol on Cyprus. He had joined the Templars some three decades before, being initiated at Beaune in Burgundy in 1265 by Humbert of Pairaud, then Master in England, and Amaury La Roche, Master in France. From what is known about him, he appears to have been very much an 'old school' Templar, being a Master who was concerned solely with the restoration of Outremer, a position in marked contrast to that of the political machinations of Guillaume de Beaujeu (but in fairness to Guillaume, the Holy Land was still in Christian hands during his tenure as Master, and de Molay faced a very different set of circumstances upon his accession to the post). De Molay supported Pope Nicholas IV's calls for a new crusade, and much of his Mastership until 1307 was concerned with trying to re-establish a Frankish presence on the mainland (the only Christian-held territory being the Templar garrison on the small island of Ruad, just off the coast from Tortosa).[27]

The Templars after 1291

With the seemingly only temporary loss of Outremer, talk was rife that the main military orders would have to merge, as the incessant bickering between the Temple and the Hospital was seen as one of the causes of the loss of the Holy Land. Neither order was keen on the idea, and the years immediately following 1291 saw the Templars, Hospitallers and Teutonic Knights trying to establish themselves in new territories and, in the case of the latter two orders, redefining their objectives. The Hospitallers cast themselves in a maritime role, making the Mediterranean their main sphere of operations. While initially based on Cyprus, in 1306 they invaded the island of Rhodes, making it their base three years later, a move that ensured them a relatively high degree of autonomy away from the interference of Rome and the kings of Europe. The Teutonics, meanwhile, decamped first to Venice and then to Marienburg in Prussia, where they devoted themselves entirely to the crusade against the pagans in the Baltic. Not only were they far away from Rome, they also fortified their position by the creation of Prussia as the *Ordensland*: this was literally a country created and run by a military order, something the Templars had long wanted to do.

The Languedoc had been the Templars' favoured location for a state of their own for some decades before the Fall of Acre, but they found themselves in the short term also on Cyprus. Although they had sold the island back to Richard the Lionheart in 1192, they had retained properties there, and Limassol became their new headquarters. However, the ghosts of the 1190s had not been entirely laid to rest, and the Order soon found itself enmeshed in local politics. King Henry of Cyprus was far from delighted to have the most powerful and feared military machine of the day arriving on his doorstep, and in 1298 he made an official complaint about the Templars' behaviour, citing the usual offences of arrogance and greed. In 1306 there was a coup, in which Henry was forced to abdicate in favour of his brother Amaury, who was supported by the Templars.

Jacques de Molay's first major undertaking as Grand Master was to travel to the West in 1294–95 to reinforce support for the Order. He arrived in Rome in December 1294, just as a new pope, Boniface VIII, was being invested. Boniface granted the Templars the same privileges in Cyprus as they had held in Outremer, which pleased Jacques de Molay, if not King Henry. Further help was at hand on the Italian peninsula: Charles II of Naples exempted the Order from paying taxes on exports of food. With such offers of help coming in, Jacques wasted no time in writing to every other monarch in Europe. He travelled to Paris and London, where Edward I promised that he would provide a crusading army once he had dealt with the French and the Scots. He also exempted the Order from paying export tax on funds that were going from the London Temple to Cyprus.

As with earlier crusades, the Templars played a central role in the build-up of a military presence in the East beginning in 1300. It was widely believed that the Mongols would return to the Holy Land, wrest Jerusalem from Mamluk control, and hand it back to the Franks. The Templars began to pave the way for a possible attack with a series of raids during the summer of 1300 on the coastal cities of Egypt and Syria, and in November they began preparations for an invasion of the mainland. Six hundred knights were sent to Ruad with orders to wait for news of the expected arrival of a combined force of Mongols under the Il-khan Ghazan and Armenians under King Hetoum. When the Mongols and Armenians did finally reach Tortosa in February 1301, they found no one there to greet them – with no sign of the reinforcements, the Templars had given up and gone back to

Cyprus. To make the situation worse, the use of Ruad in this abortive campaign had alerted the Mamluks in Egypt to the strategic importance of the island, and, in 1302, the garrison there was wiped out by a Mamluk attack. It was the loss of the very last Templar holding in Outremer.

The Arrests

The spectre of merging the Temple with the Hospital returned with the investiture of Clement V as pope in November 1305. He invited both Jacques de Molay and Fulk de Villaret, the Grand Master of the Hospital, to write and explain their views on the matter. To Jacques de Molay, the idea was untenable. In his mémoire to the Pope, dictated in 1306, he examined the case for and against a merger, and concluded that the two orders, while having similar goals, would function better if they remained independent. Clement also requested de Molay's opinion on a new crusade, to which the Grand Master responded with a second mémoire. Crusades in the past had generally been either a *passagium generale*, where everyone was free to join, such as the First Crusade, or a *passagium particulare*, in which a limited number of professional soldiers would attack a specific target, which was usually the case with most of the later crusades. De Molay went against the prevailing opinion of the time and suggested that – given the loss of Ruad – the *passagium generale* was the only viable option. Clement was not convinced, and summoned both de Molay and de Villaret to France to meet to discuss the matter further. The meeting – planned for All Saints' Day 1306 – had to be postponed when the Pope suffered an attack of gastro-enteritis. De Molay arrived in the West in either late 1306 or early 1307. Fulk de Villaret, detained by the Hospital's campaigns on Rhodes, did not arrive until late summer.

It was while de Molay and Clement were waiting for the Hospitaller Grand Master to arrive in France, that a third matter was discussed: two years earlier, allegations of gross impropriety had been made against the Templars by several knights who had been expelled, and de Molay asked the Pope to look into the matter to clear the Order's reputation. On 24 August, the Pope wrote to the French king, Philip IV, stating that he could scarcely believe the accusations made against the Order, but, as he had heard many strange things about the Templars, had decided, 'not without great sorrow, anxiety and upset of heart'[28] to instigate an inquiry. He told Philip to take no further action.

But the French king did not listen. At dawn on Friday, 13 October, his agents arrested all the Templars then in France, including Jacques de Molay, who was seized at the Temple in Paris, on charges of heresy, sodomy, blasphemy and denying Christ.

The Trial

Philip's actions caused disbelief amongst the crowned heads of Europe. James II of Aragon was not alone in believing that the charges made against the Order were trumped up, to enable the notoriously insolvent Philip to get his hands on the Templars' vast wealth. It was not the first time the French king had shocked his contemporaries with his audacity and arrogance. In 1303, he had tried to kidnap the then pope, Boniface VIII, and bring him back to France to face charges similar to those levelled at the Templars; the attempt failed, but the shock killed Boniface. Philip also mounted a long-running campaign against the Italian bankers, the Lombards, finally arresting them and stripping them of all their assets in 1311. In July 1306, the Jews had been arrested, and all their wealth had been seized before they were thrown out of the kingdom. In addition, Philip had debased the coinage several times, which had proved highly unpopular. In 1306, he had had to take refuge in the Paris Temple to escape from an angry mob, and it is possible that it was while he was inside the Templar compound that he began to scheme of finding a way to appropriate their wealth to alleviate his own, seemingly never-ending, financial problems. By the time Clement wrote to Philip in August 1307, it seems that the French king's mind was already fully made up, and the instructions to arrest the Templars went out on 14 September.

That the main charge against the Templars should be heresy suggests that, for Philip, his campaign to eradicate the Order was a personal crusade which would put him on a par with his grand-father, Louis IX (whom Boniface VIII had declared a saint in 1297 at the French king's insistence). Philip was not only an arrogant bully, he was also fanatically religious, as was the other main figure behind the arrests, the Keeper of the Seals, Guillaume de Nogaret. If anything, de Nogaret was even more of a zealot than Philip, and he is sometimes seen as the main instigator of the campaign against the Templars. (Interestingly, he is rumoured to have had a Cathar relative who died during the Albigensian Crusade – see below.) In the early fourteenth century, the fear of heresy and magic was real, and extended right the way through society, from peasants in their hovels to paranoid popes and kings. This is reflected in the heresy charges against Boniface – according to Philip and de Nogaret, the Pope was in league with the Devil – and the similar accusations levelled at the Templars.

Clement, although often seen as a weak pope who was a puppet of the French crown, did not, much to Philip's anger, comply with the campaign against the Templars. Indeed, Clement was outraged. As the Order was answerable only to

Rome, Philip's action in arresting the Templars within his domains was illegal; not only that, but de Nogaret at the time was excommunicate.[29] In an angry letter to Philip written on 27 October, Clement states that Philip has 'violated every rule' by arresting the Templars, which was a blatant 'act of contempt towards ourselves and the Roman Church'.[30] Clement's feeling that the Church itself was under threat became, for him, the real struggle that was now about to unfold.

Two days before Clement's letter to Philip, on 25 October, Jacques de Molay confessed before an assembly from the University of Paris that he had denied Christ and spat on the Cross. Other confessions followed from all the other senior Templars in captivity. There was scandal and outrage in Paris, with mobs showing their anger against the Order. This played into Philip's hands, and he renewed pressure on Clement to issue the command for Templars everywhere to be arrested. On 22 November, Clement finally acquiesced, and issued the bull *Pastoralis praeeminentiae*, which ordered the arrest of all Templars in Europe.

If Philip had hoped that other rulers would follow his example, he was very much mistaken. King James II of Aragon was incredulous, Edward II of England did as little as possible for as long as possible, in Germany there was widespread disbelief, and in Cyprus the charges were simply not believed at all. In Italy the situation varied from state to state: Naples and the Papal States acted at once, while in Lombardy, there seemed to be widespread support for the Order. Arrests were eventually made in all countries, but the success in extracting confessions depended upon whether the particular country or state allowed torture. Thus, in England and across the Iberian peninsula – where torture was either legally prohibited or used very reluctantly at the behest of Clement – very few confessions were elicited from captive Templars. In Naples and the Papal States, however, the Inquisition was allowed to use what was euphemistically known as 'ecclesiastical procedure'; the number of confessions here was, unsurprisingly, higher, although not as high as in France, where every Templar arrested – including de Molay – had been subjected to torture.

Templar confessions ranged in content, no doubt depending upon the extremities of torture applied. Most confessed to spitting, trampling and urinating on the Cross during their reception ceremony, and denying Christ on the grounds that he was a false prophet. (One Templar admitted that he had been told 'Put not thy faith in this [the crucifix], for it is too young.') The reception ceremony also included obscene kisses, usually on the navel and the base of the spine, although some confessed to kissing on the buttocks or penis. The words of consecration were said to have been omitted from the Mass. Most also confessed to worshipping an idol called Baphomet, which, depending on who was confessing at the time, was a severed head, or was one head with three faces; in other cases it was said to be the face of a bearded man, and in others, a woman or a cat. There were also admissions of having sex with demonic women, and even killing newborn children.

Clement insisted that the confessions should be heard before a Papal committee, and on 24 December, Jacques de Molay and other senior Templars appeared before it. Now seemingly safely out of the hands of Philip, de Molay retracted his confession on the grounds that he had only confessed in the first place after being tortured. The other Templars with him did likewise. Needless to say, this put a major spanner in the works of what Philip and de Nogaret had both hoped would be a swift and decisive campaign to eradicate the Order once and for all, seize its wealth and declare the French Crown the *de facto* leader of

Europe and the Defender of the One True Faith.

Clement, however, was not to be bullied, and in February 1308, suspended proceedings. Philip immediately approached doctors at the University of Paris to try to bolster the legal standing of the case for the prosecution. In their reply of 25 March, the doctors did not feel that Philip had much of a case. The King was becoming apoplectic. In May, he called a meeting of the Estates General in an attempt to win over the majority of public opinion. This too met with mixed success, and general public support for the Templars seemed to be growing alongside a distrust of the King.

Matters came to a head in June when Clement arrived at Poitiers to try to wrest control of the whole affair away from the French Crown and back into the hands of Mother Church. Philip sent 72 Templars to confess before him. On 27 June, Clement heard the confessions and agreed to set up two inquiries to handle the case: one would look at the Order as a whole; and the other would examine the case of individual Templars. That he was under virtual house arrest, with French troops sealing the town off, was without doubt a major factor in Clement's willingness to at last go along with Philip's wishes. The rest of the summer was spent in a whirlwind of bureaucracy, with summonses going out in order to get the two commissions up and running. Indeed, on one day in August, nearly 500 such letters were issued in a single day. De Molay and other Templar leaders, held at Chinon, retracted their retractions, and things at last seemed to be going Philip's way.

But it was not to be that easy. Collating all the evidence took far longer than expected, a fact which exasperated Philip, and the Papal hearings did not formally open until over a year later, on 22 November 1309. Jacques de Molay appeared before the committee on 26 November and expressed his wish to defend his Order, but felt unable to do so as he was a 'poor, unlettered knight'. Unlike the other military orders, which seemed to be much more in tune with the increasing legalism of the period, the Templars under de Molay had seemed blithely unconcerned with the changing political climate in the West, and as a result, had no legal counsel at their disposal, a fact which now appeared to be their undoing. De Molay gave further evidence two days later, and repeated that he felt unable to defend the Order. He also made a further gaffe when he announced that he would not talk to anyone but Clement in person, as he firmly believed that he could exonerate both himself and his Order with a personal appeal.

Philip's agents let imprisoned Templars know that their Grand Master had failed to defend them, in the hope that it would break their morale, and, for a while, the ploy seemed to work. However, when the hearings began again in February 1310, two Templars, Peter of Bologna and Reginald of Provins, both of whom had had legal training in the years prior to 1307, stepped forward and announced that they wished to defend their Order against all charges made against it. Philip had no choice but to allow the Templars to make their defence. On 1 April, they made a convincing case for the Order's innocence, with Peter of Bologna in particular making a powerful appeal that the Templars were not only innocent of all charges, but had been the victims of a cruel plot. He railed against the use of torture, which had merely given the Inquisitors the confessions they wished to hear (one Templar admitted that he would have even confessed to murdering God in order to stop his torments), despite the fact that they had been promised by Philip that no torture would be used.

In a move that recalled his coercion of Clement at Poitiers in June 1308, Philip now once more turned to outright bullying to get his way. On 11 May, with support growing among the imprisoned brothers for their defence, it was announced that 54 Templars who had retracted their confessions were to be burnt to death as relapsed heretics. The following day, 54 members of the Order went to the stake protesting their innocence as the flames wrapped around them. Reginald of Provins disappeared from prison, but just as mysteriously turned up again, while Peter of Bologna went missing and was never seen again. (He was probably murdered by Philip's henchmen.) The Order had no one left to defend it, and the Templar defence promptly collapsed.

The End of the Order

The fate of the Templars was to be decided at the Council of Vienne, scheduled to meet in October 1310. However, the Papal hearings dragged on, and the council had to be postponed. The hearings finally came to an end on 5 June 1311, much to Philip's relief, and the Council was able to begin its sessions on 16 October. The turn-out was low, partially due to bad weather and also due to the lack of decent accommodation in the town. After dealing with two other pressing matters – a new crusade and Church reform – the council turned its attention to dissolving the Templars. Rumour was rife that the Temple would mount a last-minute defence, and, much to everyone's surprise, seven fully armed knights who had evaded arrest four years earlier appeared to defend the Order. Clement asked the council if they should be allowed to do so, and the majority agreed that the knights should be allowed to speak.

Needless to say, Philip was enraged, and even Clement himself seems to have been surprised by the decision to let the Templars speak. The Pope wanted to end the whole matter once and for all. Disease was by now rampant in Vienne, with several churchmen having succumbed, and the thought of Philip putting in another appearance did nothing for the Pope's confidence. To add to the pressure on Clement, Philip was now threatening to break away from Rome altogether, and create an independent Church of France; the future of the church itself was at stake unless the Templar issue could be resolved, and resolved quickly.

On 20 March 1312, Philip and a small armed force did indeed arrive in Vienne, and the Pope knew that he had to act. Two days later, in a secret consistory, Clement issued the bull *Vox in excelso*, which, while not finding the Templars guilty as charged, dissolved the Order forever, such was the shame and infamy that had been brought upon it. There was still dissent among the senior clergy, with the Bishop of Valencia declaring that the suppression of the Templars was 'against reason and justice'.[31] On 2 May, a second bull, *Ad providam*, was issued, which – against Philip's wishes – transferred the Temple's possessions to the Hospital. Four days after that, a third bull, *Considerantes dudum*, gave the provincial councils the power to decide the fate of individual Templars. The fate of the Order's leaders was reserved for Papal judgment alone.

Jacques de Molay and three other senior Templars remained in prison, awaiting the Pope's decision. In late December 1313, Clement finally set up a council to decide the fate of the four men. The cardinals appointed by the Pope called for a meeting of doctors of theology and canon law to decide the matter, and the council finally met in Paris on Monday, 18 March 1314. Facing the doctors alongside Jacques de Molay were Geoffroi de Charney, Preceptor of Normandy, Hugh de Pairaud, the Order's Visitor [ambassador] in France and Geoffroi de Gonneville, Preceptor of Aquitaine and Poitou. All were old men: de Molay was at least 70; de Pairaud and de Charney were in their 60s;

while de Gonneville was probably still in his 50s. They were led out to a platform in front of Notre Dame, where the sentences were read out. As all four men stood guilty of heresy, they were condemned to 'harsh and perpetual imprisonment'.[32] Hugh de Pairaud and Geoffroi de Gonneville accepted the sentence, and were led away to die miserably in jail.

At this moment, perhaps dreading the thought of being reimprisoned (he had spent the last four years in solitary confinement), Jacques de Molay began shouting that he and his Order were innocent of all crimes, and he publicly retracted his confession. This astounded the cardinals and doctors, and they suddenly did not know what to do. After seven years of captivity, during which time he had consistently failed to defend his Order, Jacques de Molay's finest hour was suddenly at hand. He adamantly refused to confess his guilt. Geoffroi de Charney rallied to his Master, and likewise insisted on the Order's innocence. The two men were taken back to their cells while news of the unexpected turn of events was rushed to Philip. The King now had a legal and ecclesiastical emergency on his hands. He summoned the lay members of his Council and the matter was resolved. As the two Templars were insisting upon their innocence, they were guilty of being relapsed heretics, and there was only one punishment for that – death by fire.

At around the hour of Vespers, Jacques de Molay and Geoffroi de Charney were led out on to the Île aux Juifs in the Seine. In front of a crowd who had gathered to watch the two Templars in their last moments, the Grand Master and the Preceptor were stripped to their shirts. Witnesses reported that both seemed very calm, almost glad that their torment was now over. As he was fastened to the stake, de Molay asked to be turned towards the cathedral of Notre Dame, and that his hands be freed so that he could die in prayer. His request was granted. As the flames grew about him, de Molay is said to have once more protested his innocence and that of the Order, and he called both Clement and Philip to meet him before God within the year. (Philip may in fact have been watching from an upstairs window in the nearby palace.) Geoffroi de Charney likewise protested from the stake:

> 'I shall follow the way of my master
> As a martyr you have killed him
> This you have done and know not
> God willing on this day
> I shall die in the Order like him.'[33]

After nightfall, when the two men were dust and ash and the crowd had dispersed, a number of friars from the nearby Augustinian house and certain other people – who have never been identified – went to the place of execution and collected the bones of the two Templars, intent on preserving them as relics.[34]

Templar Mysteries

The fact that the Templars fell from grace so spectacularly suggests that some of the accusations against them may have had some basis in reality, or at least enough of a basis in the mediaeval imagination to render the Order's continued existence highly problematic, even had they been found innocent of the charges made against them. While many commentators – both at the time and subsequently – have seen Philip's avarice as the motivating factor behind his attack on the Order, there are those, such as the eminent mediaeval historian Sir Steven Runciman, who believe that there was a certain degree of truth to the charges: 'It would be unwise to dismiss these rumours [of heresy] as the unfounded invention of enemies. There was probably just enough substance to them to suggest the line along which the Order could be most convincingly attacked.'[35]

The guilt, or otherwise, of the Templars, has remained a contentious subject ever since. The one incontrovertible thing the trial and downfall of the Order did achieve was to add another layer of myth, one which makes discerning the 'real' Templars arguably all the more difficult. We should remind ourselves, however, that this process of mythologising the Order had been in process since their founding, and was something the Templars themselves seemed to have actively encouraged; indeed, it may have even been a contributory factor to their downfall. In this chapter, we will examine some of the main myths about the Templars. Whether they have any basis in actuality – and whether this is in itself important – will be dealt with at the end.

If the end of the Order remains controversial, then its beginnings are equally shrouded in mystery and silence.

The Mystery of Templar Origins

The traditional picture that Hugues de Payen and Godfroi de St Omer presented themselves to King Baldwin II around the year 1119 with the suggestion that they form an order of nine knights who would protect pilgrims visiting the Holy Land derives from Guillaume of Tyre (d. *c.*1186), the first chronicler to mention the Order. Yet Guillaume, like most mediaeval historians, is unreliable. He notes that the Council of Troyes was held in the ninth year of the Order's existence, which would mean that the Templars were possibly launched at the Council of Nablus in 1120, yet he also notes that they also accepted no new members for the first nine years. As Fulk, Count of Anjou, is known to have joined the Order on his pilgrimage of 1120, this would push the foundation date of the Temple back to 1111. As Runciman notes, Guillaume's dating is 'confused and at times demonstrably wrong'.[36]

If Guillaume is confused, then he is not the only one. The other two chronicles dating from the late twelfth century – those of Michael the Syrian and Walter Map – disagree not only with Guillaume, but also each other. According to Michael the Syrian (d. 1199) it was the King of Jerusalem who suggested to Hugues de Payen that he form a military order, and puts the initial membership at 30. Walter Map (d. *c.*1210) believed that the Order was founded by a knight from Burgundy called Paganus,[37] who defended pilgrims he saw frequently attacked at a horsepool near Jerusalem. Despite his best efforts, the number of infidel grew and Paganus was forced to seek extra recruits, with the knights subsequently being given lodgings near the Temple of the Lord, which could very well be the al-Aqsa mosque.

There is a further hint that the Templars were in existence before their official founding date of around 1119. Five years previously, the Bishop of Chartres had written to Hugh, Count of Champagne – himself either a founding Templar or at the very least one of the Order's first supporters – upon his return from his second visit to the East: 'We have heard that... before leaving Jerusalem you made a vow to join the Militia of Christ, that you will enrol in this evangelical soldiery.'[38] As the phrase 'Militia of Christ' would also be employed by St Bernard in reference to the Templars, and given the close ties between Hugh, Bernard and the fledgling Order, it is this comment from the Bishop of Chartres that is perhaps the most persuasive evidence we have that the Templars – in one form or another – existed at least as early as 1114.

The air of mystery that surrounds the Temple's early years is compounded by the fact that the years before the Council of Troyes are the Order's least documented period. Indeed, they are hardly documented at all. The Templars themselves had no official records of their foundation, which is unusual for a religious order. There were no Western chroniclers in Outremer until the time of the Second Crusade and, more remarkably, the King's chronicler, Fulk de Chartres, who was living in Jerusalem at the time of the Order's supposed foundation, does not mention them at all. There are only four documents existing prior to the Council of Troyes that make note of the Templars, two of them mentioning the Order in connection with the Hospital.[39] A later chronicle – that of Ernoul and Bernard the Treasurer – also suggests that there was some kind of close link between the two orders. Interestingly, in this version the Templars 'asked the king to give them his palace in front of the Lord's Temple'.[40] Indeed, recent research[41] seems to confirm that the Templars were initially given accommodation by the Augustinian Canons of the Church of the Holy Sepulchre, and that the buildings they occupied were part of the Hospital, which lay just to the south.

So if the Templars were originally based at the Hospital – and possibly as early as 1111 – what where they doing? Out of the four pre-1129 documents, none of them describes the Templars as protecting pilgrims. Could they have been simply providing security at the Hospital, or was something else going on? It has frequently been asserted[42] that the Templars were part of some grand design that was inaugurated with the First Crusade. While this cannot be proved, it cannot be disproved either. Sufficient gaps exist in the historical record to allow the Templars a more nebulous role than that with which they have been traditionally ascribed. Certainly there were shady characters whose names have not come down to us who were moving in the background in the early years of Outremer. Godfroi de Bouillon, for instance, was accompanied to the East by a group of near-anony-mous advisers, the only one of whom whose name is known being Peter the Hermit. Peter was possibly linked to a mysteri-ous group of monks who arrived on Godfroi's estates at Orval in the Ardennes sometime around 1090, having travelled en masse from Calabria in Italy. Peter is then thought to have become Godfroi's personal tutor and, in 1095, was one of those who called for a Crusade. (Indeed, Peter actually led the first band of Crusaders to leave Europe.) When Jerusalem fell, Godfroi was offered the crown of Jerusalem by a group of mysterious nobles, who included 'a certain bishop of Calabria', and Godfroi then seems to have had an abbey built just outside the city walls, on

Mount Sion. The resulting Order of Sion is one of the most obscure religious fraternities of the period, and it has been suggested that it is from this group that the Templars derived.[43] Another contender for the title of 'the order behind the Order' is the network of families from whom the original Templars were descended. All of these families were from the Champagne/ Burgundy regions of France and have been dubbed the 'Troyes fraternity'.[44] The Templars would therefore have been agents of this fraternity, originally loyal to them before papal support forced the Order to be officially subservient to Rome. A further theory posits the Cluniacs as the power behind the throne, given that they were extremely wealthy and avidly pro-Crusade.[45] Whichever position one inclines towards, it is certain that the early Templars were well connected and enjoyed the patronage of powerful men well before official recognition at the Council of Troyes.

Hugh, Count of Champagne, is an even more interesting figure than Godfroi and, like him, arguably had direct links to the 'order behind the Order'. His departure for the East in 1104 seems to have been at the behest of a group of anonymous nobles and it is possible that Hugh visited Outremer on some kind of fact-finding mission. By the time of his second visit in 1114, the Militia of Christ – quite possibly the Templars – had been formed. Although Hugh did not join immediately, he returned to France and donated land to St Bernard, who used it to found the new monastic house of Clairvaux. St Bernard later became the Templars' chief apologist in the West; the Cistercians and the Templars expanded at an exponential rate and at roughly the same time, with Hugh supporting both Orders. Was Hugh working in accord with some larger plan, or was he simply a pious man who was doing what pious, wealthy men did in those days to ensure that his soul would fare well in the next world?

Despite his piety and wealth, Hugh, when he did officially join the Templars in 1125, had to swear an oath of fealty, as would any new recruit to the Order. This meant swearing an oath of fealty to Hugues de Payen, which, in Hugh's case, meant that he was taking the highly unusual step of swearing an oath to one of his own vassals. This is remarkable in itself and could suggest that, even at this early stage, there was a powerful mystique surrounding the Order.

The Temple and the Temple Mount

One tradition holds that while officially supposed to be protecting pilgrims, the Templars – or a group of them, at least – were involved in archaeological excavations that took place beneath the Temple platform, in what are known as Solomon's Stables. There had long been rumours that the treasure of the Second Temple, which was destroyed in the conflagration of 70 AD, was hidden beneath the Temple Mount and it is possible that Hugues de Payen, Hugh of Champagne and others knew of this and undertook to find it. This could be a possible reason for the Order specifically asking to be based at the al-Aqsa mosque; the idea of being based on the supposed site of King Solomon's Temple – with its repository of secrets and wisdom – would have no doubt been a further lure, an example of the Templars themselves being seduced by a myth. If the Templars were not actively excavating, then they could have stumbled across something in the stables while undertaking alterations, as they were known to have carried out a great deal of building work around the al-Aqsa mosque, starting from the 1120s, work that was still in progress even when Jerusalem fell to Saladin in 1187.

Various excavations, beginning with the Warren expedition of 1867, have found numerous tunnels beneath the Temple Mount and in 1968 an Israeli team discovered a tunnel dubbed 'the Templar tunnel', which is thought to lead directly under the Dome of the Rock. Another team reopened one of Warren's tunnels in 1981, but a group of Muslim protesters, fearing that the Israelis would use the tunnel to access the Dome of the Rock, managed to prevent any further work. The tunnel remains sealed to this day.[46]

If the Order did indeed find something beneath the Temple Mount, what could it have been? Speculation has been rife (indeed, where the Templars are concerned, speculation is always rife) that they found one or more priceless relics, from the embalmed head of John the Baptist to documents pertaining to the true origins of Christianity – proof that Jesus survived the Crucifixion, was married to and had a family with Mary Magdalene or that the real Messiah was the Baptist – and/or the Ark of the Covenant. Then again, maybe they had unearthed the treasure of the Second Temple, which was known to have been comprised of gold and other precious metals and stones. That a major find of this sort could have occurred is not beyond the realms of possibility; after all, the texts discovered at Nag Hammadi and Qumran in the mid-to-late 1940s had lain untouched and well preserved for almost 2,000 years and neither discovery was the result of deliberate excavation. (Indeed, it is from one of the Dead Sea Scrolls – the Copper Scroll – that we know what the Temple treasure was comprised of.)

The theory then holds that, armed with their discovery, the Templars were subsequently able to blackmail the Church into silence in return for wealth and power. This would, of course, give the Church ample reason to pursue the downfall of the Order – a downfall they would have to wait nearly two centuries to see. This version of the story implies that the Council of

Troyes was effectively a smoke-screen, and that the real reasons for the Templars' astounding expansion in the years immediately following it can be ascribed not to the Order tapping into the era's pious zeitgeist, but to whatever it was they found buried under the Temple Mount. The twelfth century was not kind to the Church and Rome would have been in no position to do anything other than acquiesce to anyone presenting evidence that the whole basis of their worldly power was in fact a house built on sand. Indeed, it would not be until the election of the great reforming pope, Innocent III, in 1198 that the Papacy started to regain much-needed ground. Interestingly, it was Innocent who accused the Templars of necromancy. Did he know something about the Order, or was he merely using the most forceful terminology of the day to make the Templars toe the Church's line? Or was it a case of both?

The Temple and the Grail

Some versions of the excavation theory suggest that the Templars found nothing less than the Holy Grail, the one priceless relic with which the Templars are most closely associated. In popular chivalric epics of the period, such as Wolfram von Eschenbach's *Parzival*, the Templars are portrayed as its guardians. Another grail romance, the thirteenth-century French romance *Perlesvaus*, may have actually been written by a Templar, such is its attention to detail in regard to military matters and the fact that it features knights who wear the Templar mantle of the red cross on the white background. Perhaps significantly, one of the knights, referred to as a 'master', claims to have seen the Grail.

Quite why the Templars were portrayed as the guardians of the Grail is a mystery. They were known to have practised an unusual rite on Holy Thursday 'that seems to be connected to the legend of the Holy Grail',[47] and there is at least one other plausible link that connects the Order to the Grail romances: the city in which the Order was officially launched, Troyes, is also the city in which the first Grail romance was written. The *Conte del Graal* was written by Chrétien de Troyes around 1180. Chrétien claimed that he had based his poem on a book given to him by his patron, Philip of Flanders, who had campaigned in the East alongside the Templars during the late 1170s and could have conceivably heard the story from them. While claiming that one's work was based on an earlier source was a fairly common literary device of the time, we also can't be certain that Philip *didn't* give Chrétien a text he had acquired in the East.

A slightly later version of the Grail story, Wolfram von Eschenbach's *Parzival* (composed *c.*1220) makes the Eastern connection more explicit by setting some of his poem there (he personally visited Outremer around 1200), and by peppering his text with esoteric references that may have come about through contact with the more mystically inclined elements in the Muslim world.

The link between the Templars and the Grail does not, of course, bring us any closer to understanding what the Grail actually is. Chrétien refers not to '*the* Grail' but '*a* Grail' and compounded the mystery by dying before he could finish his poem. Robert de Boron, who is thought to have visited Cyprus and may therefore have moved in Templar circles, was the first writer expressly to Christianise the Grail; he also made it the *Holy* Grail. Both of these versions of the Grail story appear to be Christianised versions of the Celtic Cauldron of Plenty, which is said to have granted fertility to the land and to have been an endless source of renewal. Wolfram von Eschenbach agrees that the Grail is capable of these things, but describes the Grail not as the traditional cup used at the Last Supper, but as a stone called *lapsis exillis*. In Wolfram's hands, the Grail sounds similar to the Philosopher's Stone, the gaining of which was the goal of alchemy, and alchemical secrets were finding their way into Europe at around this time through contact with the East.

Perhaps the most well-known modern theory about the Grail, such as that proposed in the book *The Holy Blood and the Holy Grail*, suggests that the Grail is in fact Jesus's bloodline, which continued through his marriage to Mary Magdalene and their offspring, who eventually intermarried with the Merovingian dynasty. The hypothesis further holds that Godfroi de Bouillon himself had Merovingian blood flowing in his veins, so therefore his crowning as Defender of the Holy Sepulchre in 1099 would have made the Church profoundly uneasy. As the Church was said to have colluded in the assassination of the last Merovingian king, Dagobert II, in 679, Godfroi's coronation becomes much more symbolic than being merely the end process of a barbarous military campaign; it is nothing less than the retrieval of Jerusalem in the name of the real Christ and the Magdalene, not the Church. The Templars, being in on the secret, were set up to protect the continued safety of the blood-line; any hypothetical discovery under the Temple Mount would have only served to strengthen the Templars' reputation as possessors of secrets, as well as confirming their supposed position as being hostile to the Church. This would of course have provided another reason for the Church to want the Templars destroyed.

Regardless of which version of the Grail myth one subscribes to – and it has been suggested that there are as many Grails as there are seekers[48] – they are all, with the debatable exception of the bloodline theory, allegories of the spiritual path. If certain elements within the Templars were indeed drawn towards mysticism and forms of spirituality and knowledge that were outside of official Church doctrine, then connecting the Order with the Grail romances makes an associative sense, both being concerned with inner illumination and progress towards the Divine. Troyes, for instance, had a Cabalistic school that was active from around 1070 and some of the Grail romances can certainly be interpreted along Cabalistic lines. Given the Templars' close links with Troyes, it is not beyond the realms of possibility that they could have absorbed some of this thinking.

The Temple and the Arab World

It was after the failure of the Second Crusade that rumours began to circulate that the Templars had deliberately sabotaged the Crusade through their treacherous alliances with the infidel. The anonymous Würzburg annalist believed that the Templars had accepted a massive bribe from Unur, the ruler of Damascus at the time of the campaign, to engineer the retreat which led to the failure of the Crusade. Although accusations like these betray the usual inability of Western chroniclers to grasp the complexities of the situation in the East, where some form of accommodation between the Franks and Islam was a practical necessity, the Templars' reputation does seem to have been tarnished from this time on (at least in the eyes of their critics in the West).

As has been noted, the Templars often employed Muslim secretaries and a number of the Order learnt Arabic. Similarly, they had a good, albeit unpredictable, relationship with the Assassins, who are often seen as the Islamic equivalent of the Templars. The Order also came into contact with the Sufis. It is plausible, therefore, that ideas from the Islamic world found their way back to Europe via the Order. Twelfth-century Moorish Spain, for instance, acted in precisely this way, with a vast amount of learning coming into Europe via places like the

University of Toledo, which had a school entirely devoted to translating works from the Arabic. This influx of knowledge had an incalculable effect on the West; indeed, it would not be too much of an overstatement to suggest that one of the most important things in the intellectual development of the West was the discovery of the East, Arabic culture and science being far in advance of the West at this time.

The Templars 'through their sustained and sympathetic contact with Islamic and Judaic culture came to act as a clearing-house for new ideas, new dimensions of knowledge, new sciences'.[49] Partially as a result of this influx of knowledge, this resulted in the Templars being at the forefront of developments in all spheres: they had the best armourers, leather-workers, stonemasons, military architects and engineers. Not only that, but the Order 'contributed to the development of surveying, map-making, road-building and navigation. They possessed their own sea-ports, shipyards and fleet – a fleet both commercial and military, which was among the first to use the magnetic compass. And as soldiers, the Templars' need to treat wounds and illness made them adept in the use of drugs'.[50] Templar medicine certainly benefited from contact with the Arab doctors and through them the Order learnt how to use a primitive form of antibiotics in the shape of mould extract. The Templars' medical skill extended to their horses as well: the Order had the very best veterinarians of the day.

The Templars also enjoyed contact with various Jewish scholars. As we have noted, there was a Cabalistic school in Troyes and Jewish scholars were often prevailed upon to assist with translating duties. Again, Moorish Spain was the locus of much of this wisdom. There, the Templars 'are believed to have come into contact with those who were well-versed in geometry, astronomy, alchemical philosophy, Kabbala and mathematics'.[51]

With such close contact with not only the Arab world, but also Judaism, it is hardly surprising that the Templars were seen to be fraternising with the enemy and such contact may have contributed in a large part to the Templars' alleged religious heterodoxy.

The Temple and Heresy

Religious heterodoxy nearer home may also have been tainting Templar thought. The Order has long been associated with the Cathars, the heretical dualist sect which flourished in the twelfth and thirteenth centuries, mainly in southern France and parts of northern Italy. Alarmed at the spread of the heresy, Pope Innocent III proclaimed a Crusade against it in 1208. This was the so-called Albigensian Crusade, named after the French town of Albi, which was a stronghold of Catharism. Under men such as Simon de Montfort, the crusade quickly became notorious for its cruelty and violence; in two decades, it reduced the Languedoc to a wasteland. If that was not enough, the Inquisition was then established to root out the remaining Cathars, with their last major stronghold at Montségur falling to the forces of Louis IX in 1244. It was also, significantly, a crusade that the Templars refused to take part in.

The Templars had not participated in the Fourth Crusade on the grounds that it was not a crusade against the infidel but against fellow Christians (despite Jerusalem being its goal, it ended up sacking Constantinople instead), and this is usually seen as being the reason that the Order did not assume a role in the crusade against the Cathars. However, while the majority of Templars would have been simple, unlettered men who adhered to the Catholic Church, there may possibly have been elements within the Order sympathetic to Catharism. Bertrand de

Blancfort, the sixth Grand Master of the Temple, was said to have come from a Cathar family and the Order welcomed Cathars into its ranks once the Albigensian Crusade was under way. So great was the number of Cathar Templars in the Languedoc that, in many preceptories, Cathars outnumbered Catholics. The Order had always accepted excommunicates – the reason for this being usually cited as the constant manpower shortage in the East – but the same cannot be said for the Order's sheltering of Cathars in the West, where the manpower situation was nowhere near as dire. This apparent friendliness towards the Cathars could be a legacy of Bertrand de Blancfort, but it could also reflect the Order's desire to maintain its standing within the Languedoc, where it enjoyed a great deal of political support. The Order may have even considered the Languedoc as the most likely site for the official creation of their own *Ordensland*. Indeed, such was the Templars' strength in this region, that it was effectively a Templar *Ordensland* in all but name.

Catharism is often regarded as a mediaeval resurgence of Gnosticism, the ancient tradition that stressed *gnosis*, or direct inner knowledge, of God. Proscribed by the early Church, Gnosticism had all but disappeared by the fourth century, but certain Gnostic schools managed to survive. One such group was the Mandaeans, who revered John the Baptist above Jesus. It has been suggested that Hugues de Payen himself subscribed to the Johannite beliefs of the Mandaeans and the Order is known to have held John the Baptist in particularly high regard. The origins for this are obscure, but it could be linked to the Templars' putative original base at the Hospital: around 1100, the Hospitallers, originally known as the Hospital of Jerusalem of John the Almoner, became – for reasons unknown – the Hospital of Jerusalem of John the Baptist.[52] Gnosticism also has links with Cabala and Hermeticism, both of which the Templars could have become exposed to while in the East.

Another school of thought holds that the Templars were linked with the cult of Mary Magdalene, who was (along with John the Baptist) a particular favourite of the Order. The cult of the Virgin Mary was at its height in the twelfth century and the Virgin was also the Templars' patroness. The two Marys are traditionally seen as the feminine face of God. St Bernard himself was obsessed with the Divine Feminine and, given his close relationship to the Templars, may have either transmitted a reverence for the Feminine to the Order, or have developed his fascination at the same time that certain members of the Templars did theirs. One must not forget also that Europe at this time was undergoing rapid changes (the so-called Renaissance of the Twelfth Century), and it is a curious fact that explosions of interest in the Goddess tend to recur at times of great change and enquiry. So, this raises the question: were some of the Templars secret Goddess worshippers? Or is that merely a contemporary misreading of mediaeval devotion to the Divine Feminine in the persons of the Virgin and the Magdalene?

Pope Innocent III certainly thought that the Templars were worshipping something other than the God of the New Testament and his only Son, when he admonished the Order in his letter of 1208. He accused them of the usual sins of pride and arrogance – accusations which date back at least as far as the Second Crusade, when rumours of the Order's alliance with Islam were beginning to circulate – but also branded them necromancers who were in danger of doing the Devil's work unless they got their house in order. That the Pope himself should be moved to admit that there was something altogether not right about the Templars suggests that rumours of the Order being tainted with heresy may well have had some basis in fact. At the very least, it suggests an antinomian tendency within the

Order: it is often overlooked that the Council of Troyes, before approving the Templars, also ordered them to drop certain unorthodox practices. What these practices were has never come to light.

The Head of the Templars

Charges of Devil worship notoriously resurfaced a century later, during the Order's trial at the hands of Philip IV. This seven-year period is possibly the best documented in the Order's history, as well as being the one period in which their alleged unorthodox beliefs were at the centre of interest. The French prosecutors homed in on two areas of Templar practice: the initiation ceremony and the fact that they were supposed to worship an idol named Baphomet.

At the initiation ceremony, it was alleged, the new brothers had to show their loyalty to the Order by spitting, trampling or urinating on the Cross and by denying Christ. These have traditionally been seen as charges trumped up by Philip, but the discovery in the Vatican Library of what is known as the Chinon Parchment in 2001 confirms that the Templars did indeed spit on the Cross and deny Christ. When under questioning at Chinon in the summer of 1308, Jacques de Molay explained that these apparently sacrilegious practices were designed to force the new Templar to experience the sort of torture he would likely receive whilst in the hands of the Saracens, to deny his religion 'with the mind only and not with the heart'.[53] When one recalls that some of the evidence against the Templars was collected by 12 of Philip's spies, who joined the Order in 1306 to substantiate the allegations made the year before by the expelled knight Esquin de Floyran, it suggests that the charges against the Order were in fact true, but the purpose of these ceremonies had been misunderstood by Philip's men.

Misunderstanding is almost certainly at the root of the allegation that the Templars worshipped an idol called Baphomet. Descriptions of it varied, but it was usually described as being a life-sized head, which was said to make the land fertile (as is said of the Grail). That the Templars did possess heads is without doubt: they had the head of St Euphemia of Chalcedon at their preceptory in Nicosia on Cyprus and, more curiously, a silver head-shaped reliquary was found after the arrests at the Paris Temple. It bore the inscription CAPUT LVIII and inside it were parts of a woman's skull (who was believed to have been one of the 11,000 virgins martyred at Cologne with St Ursula). The heads may have indeed been worshipped, in the way that the Celts revered the head. The Assassins, during their initiation ceremonies, buried the initiate up to his neck in sand, leaving only the head visible, before disinterring him; given their simulation of Saracen torture, the Templars may also have carried out this practice. A further possibility is that Baphomet, long thought to be a mistranslation of 'Mahomet' (that is, the Prophet Muhammad), could well be a corruption of the Arabic word *abufihamat*, which means 'Father of Understanding', a reference to a spiritual seeker after realisation or enlightenment has taken place. 'The Baphomet', wrote the Sufi scholar Idries Shah, 'is none other than the symbol of the completed man.'[54] It is therefore possible that the supposed head the Templars were alleged to have worshipped was actually a metaphorical head. This seems to be confirmed by the findings of the Biblical scholar Hugh Schonfield, who applied the so-called 'Atbash cipher' to the word 'Baphomet': the result was the word 'wisdom'. That Hugues de Payen's shield bore three black heads suggests that certain elements within the Order – the upper echelons, perhaps – could have been familiar with esoteric disciplines learned from the Sufis from the very beginning of the Temple's existence, a theory given possible weight by the fact that, as we have noted, the Order was ordered to drop certain unorthodox practices as early as the Council of Troyes in 1129. Alternatively, the Order could have developed a reverence for the wisdom symbolised by the head through contact with Gnostic groups, who revered wisdom in the person of Sophia, the youngest emanation of the Divine and the feminine face of the true God.

However, the Baphomet is not the only head with which the Templars are linked. The thirteenth-century panel painting of a strange head discovered in Templecombe in Somerset – the Order's West of England headquarters – in 1945 has led some commentators to believe that the Templars also possessed the Turin Shroud,[55] the supposed burial cloth of Christ. The Templecombe head does indeed bear some resemblance to the face on the Shroud, and 'there is clear evidence of the existence of an unusual image of Christ in the religious life of the order'.[56] What this image was scholars are still researching, but it may possibly have been an image of Christ as the Man of Sorrows, which bears some resemblance to the face on the Shroud, hence the origins of the theory.

Interestingly, the first family to exhibit the Shroud – in 1357 – were the de Charnys, who were directly related (despite the slight difference in the spelling of the name) to Geoffroi de Charney, the Preceptor of Normandy who died with de Molay at the stake. Theories hold that the Shroud was among the many relics taken from Constantinople during the carnage inflicted on the city by the Fourth Crusade in 1204, subsequently making its way back to Europe where it ended up in the possession of the Templars. In 1357, Margaret, the widow of Geoffroi de Charny (c.1300–56) – who was a nephew of his illustrious near-namesake, the Preceptor of Normandy – had the Shroud publicly exhibited in the church at Lirey. This 1357 exposition is usually regarded as the earliest 'sighting' of the Turin Shroud, which was sold in the fifteenth century to the wealthy Italian family of Savoy, who owned it until 1983, when they relinquished control to the Church. Critics still debate whether the de Charny shroud was ever in Constantinople and whether the Templars ever actually possessed it, as there is no reference to the Shroud during their trial. All we can say for certain is that Geoffroi was related to the Templars by blood; that he was a member of a short-lived order modelled on the Templars called the Order of the Star; and that Lirey was in the diocese of Troyes.

Mysteries in Stone

That the Temple possessed relics is beyond doubt; it is one area in which they appear to be at their most orthodox. What continues to provoke speculation is, of course, *what* relics the Order had in its possession. Other theories hold that the Order also embodied sacred wisdom in stone through its programme of building, which began almost as soon as it moved onto the Temple Mount around 1120. As with relics, the notion of sacred buildings having a sacred meaning woven into their fabric is not particularly unorthodox, unless of course that meaning deviates from official Church doctrine. The Templars' round churches have long been a source of fascination in this area. They are also claimed to have been involved in the building of the first Gothic cathedrals, as well as having had connections with Rosslyn Chapel in Scotland. As is the case with much Templar mythology, there are some facts scattered in amongst a great deal of conjecture.

The Templars did not invent round churches and it is probable that their interest in this unusual form of church design was influenced by the Church of the Holy Sepulchre – near the Order's original headquarters – which has a rotunda. Originally built in the fourth century by the Emperor Constantine, this church was badly damaged in 614 and 1009; the rotunda had been rebuilt by 1048, and the Templars themselves oversaw further reconstruction and rededication in 1149. The importance of the rotunda lay in its housing of the tomb of Christ, a reminder of the true purpose of the Crusades, and therefore of the Order itself. Today, only a few Templar round churches remain – Temple Church in London being one of the most notable.[57]

Round churches were rare in Europe, although other orders – notably the Hospitallers – also built them. The Church favoured the more orthodox cruciform layout, with the result that round churches came to have a vague whiff of heresy about them – perhaps an echo of the theory that the Templars' real inspiration for building round churches was not the Church of the Holy Sepulchre at all, but the rotunda of the Dome of the Rock (known to the crusaders as the Temple of the Lord). Once the Templars had relocated to the al-Aqsa mosque, the Dome of the Rock was on their doorstep and they would have had plenty of opportunity to study the building's design. Then again, perhaps the Templars were inspired by both, a further reflection of their tendency to blend Eastern influences with Western.[58]

The influence of the East is apparent in Gothic architecture, which began to appear across Europe shortly after the Templars arrived on their campaigning tour in the late 1120s, a fact which has led some to speculate that the Templars were behind the creation of such masterpieces as Chartres and Notre Dame in Paris. As with many Templar myths, there is a partial degree of truth to this: returning crusaders – Templars among them – did bring back a great deal of learning from the East and some of these new ideas did inform subsequent building practices in the West, such as the development of the pointed arch, improvements in the production of stained glass and in various decorative motifs. The Order had its own masons, but as these mason-brothers do not seem to have been obliged to work solely for the Order, they were able to work on non-Templar projects and could therefore have been employed in the construction of certain Gothic buildings. (One of the more unlikely theories proposes that the Templars were able to fund the construction of the cathedrals through various mining and trading activities in the New World; for more on which, see below.) In all probability, the Templars would have provided as much support as they could, but this was almost certainly not financial: all the money from their properties in the West went East and there was little if any surplus cash available to be diverted into costly endeavours such as the building of a cathedral.

Rosslyn Chapel has even less direct connection with the Templars, as the foundation stone was not laid until 1446, nearly a century and a half after the end of the Order. However, a connection of sorts is there: the chapel's founder (and funder) was Sir William St Clair, grandson of Prince Henry Sinclair,[59] Earl of Orkney, who was reputed to have sailed as far as the New World in 1398, possibly using Templar charts to guide him (see below). The Order's first Grand Master, Hugues de Payen, was also known to have visited the area in 1128 – possibly because he was alleged to have been married to a Sinclair before he founded the Templars – and the Order was given land at nearby Balantradoch (now known as Temple), which became its Scottish headquarters. A further fragile link is provided by the fact that Sir William, while himself not a Templar, was a member of the Order of Santiago, which welcomed former Templars after the suppression of 1312.

The chapel is perhaps most famous for being the alleged resting place of one or more priceless relics: the Holy Grail, the embalmed heads of Jesus and/or John the Baptist and the Ark of the Covenant have all at one time or another been thought to lie inside or under the celebrated Apprentice Pillar, or slumbering in a lost vault beneath the building. It goes without saying that the Order was said to have found one or more of these relics under the Temple Mount in Jerusalem, in one of the Holy Places, or in the much-fabled town of Rennes-le-Château in the Templar heartland of the Languedoc.

The chapel's famously enigmatic carvings are thought by some to embody esoteric Templar wisdom, much of which was later adopted by Templarist Freemasons, who make much of the alleged secrets contained in Rosslyn's multifarious stonework. While it is true that the chapel contains much that is pagan – there are more than 100 green men and women at Rosslyn – these symbols are not exclusively Templar. However, one statue appears to be of the Templar seal: two knights riding the same horse. In addition, the reliefs of plants unknown in Europe at the time, possibly maize and aloe, hint that the Templars or their descendants reached the New World. These claims, as with much else in the Templar mythos, exist in that strange, liminal space between myth and history, probably never to be proved, but nor entirely disproved either. Despite its tangential nature to the Templars, Rosslyn remains a breathtaking building, a place of genuine beauty and tranquillity.

Stonework of a different – and much humbler – sort could arguably be the Templars' most enigmatic architectural legacy. The dungeons of Chinon Castle, where de Molay and the other Templar leaders were held in the summer of 1308, contain a number of highly singular carvings, thought to have been executed by one or more of the imprisoned brethren. Splayed hands revealing hearts, what appear to be dividers, double-headed axes and various geometrical grids and crosses arguably suggest an unorthodox spirituality. Similar carvings can also be found in the dungeons of Lincoln Castle, where English Templars were imprisoned at around the same time, and at Royston Cave in Hertfordshire, which has long had Templar associations. These odd, almost unnoticeable markings represent some tangible evidence that the Templars could indeed have possessed secrets, but they remain undeciphered to this day.

The Templars After 1314

The eminent nineteenth-century Catholic theologian and historian Ignaz Dollinger was once asked what he thought was the most evil day in history. He did not hesitate in his reply: it was Friday, 13 October 1307, the day the Templars were arrested in France.[60] It was felt at the time that the arrests were a criminal act of unparalleled dimensions. Dante compared Philip IV to Pontius Pilate and charged him with avarice in the *Purgatorio* (Canto XX), and the subsequent myths surrounding the Templars got off to a very quick start: Clement died only a month after Jacques de Molay had called him to account before God within the year, while Philip himself died on 29 November 1314 in a hunting accident, deaths which were attributed to what became known as the Curse of Jacques de Molay. The Curse is also said to have been responsible for the premature deaths of Philip's sons, all of whom died without male issue, bringing the Capetian dynasty to an end within a generation.

Although the trial and suppression had succeeded in destroying the Order of the Temple, it failed in other areas. Philip did not find the Templars' treasure and most of the Order's lands ended up being passed on to the Hospital. It is also unclear just how many Templars were actually arrested (the figures range between 2,000 and 15,000), and it is likewise uncertain as to how many escaped. Certainly the Order seems to have received some kind of tip-off: shortly before the events of 13 October, Jacques de Molay recalled all the Order's rulebooks and accounts and had them burnt. A brother who left the Order in 1307 was told that he was 'wise', as an unspecified catastrophe was looming. A memo was circulated to all French preceptories forbidding them from releasing any information about the Order's rites and rituals.[61]

If the Order knew what Philip's plans were in advance, that might explain why the French King was unable to find the Order's treasure (assuming it to have been actual, rather than metaphorical), which was said to have been smuggled out of the Paris Temple shortly before the arrests and taken by river to the Templars' nautical base at the port of La Rochelle. How many Templar ships sailed from La Rochelle in the autumn of 1307 is unknown – what they were carrying likewise – but one thing is known: the Templar fleet vanished utterly. Alternative theories hold that the ships leaving from La Rochelle were merely a decoy, with the main escape happening from Aragon.[62]

If the Order did indeed have some kind of advance warning and an unknown number of Templars escaped, where did they go and what did they do? Although the Order of the Temple ceased to exist in 1312, Templars did not and various theories have been proposed as to their subsequent fate.

The Temple and the New World

Some Templars were welcomed into the Hospital, while others joined the Teutonic Knights. It was on the Iberian Peninsula, however, that the Templars managed to effect the most successful survival. In Spain, the Order of Montesa was created 'primarily as a refuge for fugitive Templars',[63] while in Portugal, King Diniz found the Order innocent of all crimes and the Templars there simply changed their name to the Knights of Christ. Under this name, they became heavily involved in exploration and numerous theories propose that the Templars were now able to capitalise on the nautical skills they had acquired during the official existence of the Order. We know that the Templars had their own fleet by the early thirteenth century, with their main sea base being at Marseilles and, by 1301, the fleet had its own admiral, suggesting that it had, by this time, become a small navy. The exact size of the Templar fleet, however, has never been established. It is known that the Hospitallers owned only a handful of ships, simply hiring other vessels when they had need of them. As this was also standard practice at the time for everyone from traders to kings, it is probable that the Templars did the same. When not on official Templar business, their ships possibly engaged in what amounted to licensed piracy, and one powerful Templar captain, Roger de Flor (d. 1305), was even thought to have lent his name to the pirate flag, the Jolly Roger. He fell foul of de Molay, however, who accused Roger of looting during the evacuation from Acre in 1291, expelling him from the Order. Undeterred, Roger founded the Grand Catalan Company and continued as a Templar agent.

With such a murky naval reputation, it comes as no surprise to learn that, according to some theories, the Templars, in their new guise as Knights of Christ, accompanied Henry Sinclair on his 1398 voyage, during which they reached North America, landing in Nova Scotia and later getting as far as Massachusetts and Rhode Island, where they may have been responsible for the building of the Newport Tower and the carving of the effigy known as the Westford Knight. However, the text detailing this alleged voyage – the so-called Zeno Narrative – was not written until 1558 and is widely regarded as being highly spurious.

Another legend that links the Templars with the New World is that of the mystery of Oak Island in Nova Scotia and its so-called Money Pit. In 1795 a shaft was said to have been discovered on the island and several years later an inscription was unearthed that claimed the shaft contained buried treasure. Various attempts have been made over the years to excavate the Money Pit, costing several people their lives, but so far no one has been able to locate whatever is buried in the pit – if anything – or to determine whether the Money Pit is actually an artificial construction, complete with elaborate flood traps, or is in fact a natural formation. One theory, among many, suggests that the Templars, after having crossed the Atlantic with Henry Sinclair, buried their lost treasure there, or possibly even the Grail itself. (Other theories, incidentally, claim that the Money Pit contains Sir Francis Drake's jewels, Captain Kidd's gold, or proof that Sir Francis Bacon wrote the complete works of Shakespeare.)

Despite the fringe nature of these claims, there is in fact a slightly more tangible connection between the Templars and North America. Both Prince Henry the Navigator and Vasco da Gama were Knights of Christ (Henry was actually a Grand Master), as was Christopher Columbus's father-in-law. Moreover, Columbus was known to have used navigators on his 1492 expedition who also belonged to the Order. The charts they used were said to have been handed down through generations of Knights of Christ, which, if that were indeed the case, begs the question, how extensive were the charts and at what point did the Knights of Christ acquire that knowledge? Had they actually reached the New World at some point prior to 1492 and, if so, when? Could they have inherited some of this knowledge from Templar captains like Roger de Flor? Despite his colourful career, it is highly unlikely that Roger ever made it across the Atlantic, although some theories hold that the Templars had not only reached America long before Roger's time, but also set up successful mining and trading operations there, the profits from which went back to Europe to fund various enterprises.

The theory that the Templars discovered America is probably the result of confusion between the original Templars and their Portuguese successors. If any 'Templars' could be said to have discovered America, it was – by way of Columbus – the Knights of Christ. Such tenuous links are common in Templar mythology, but, before we scotch the New World theories completely, we should remember that the discovery of America, and the subject of pre-Columbian voyages to the New World generally, continues to be a controversial area. And Columbus himself remains something of an enigma: his nationality has been disputed and, perhaps significantly, his ships bore a red cross on their sails very similar to the Templar cross.

The Temple and the Lodge

As we have noted, the fate of the Templar fleet – whatever its size – has never been resolved. Almost the only place the ships could have found a safe haven would have been western Scotland, then under the control of Robert the Bruce. This theory is explored at length by Michael Baigent and Richard Leigh in their book *The Temple and the Lodge*, which proposes that a contingent of Templars landed in Argyll, helped Bruce win the Battle of Bannockburn and then continued to reside in Scotland relatively unmolested. All the Scottish Templars escaped arrest; the only two members of the Order to be arrested there were in fact English, both of whom were acquitted. Baigent and Leigh argue that, while the Papal Bull *Ad providam* ordered the transfer of Templar property to the Hospital, in Scotland this process seems to have dragged on much longer than elsewhere, with the Hospitallers not gaining control of some Templar properties until the 1340s. The Scottish Templars and their descendants were therefore still active, if keeping a somewhat low profile. Some of them, Baigent and Leigh argue, could possibly have been members of the Scots Guard, an allegedly Templarist organisation which was founded in 1425 and was sworn to protect the French monarch. Eventually, some of its members returned to Scotland, where they were to play a part in the founding of Freemasonry. (One family whose sons served in the Scots Guard was the Sinclairs, of Rosslyn Chapel fame.)

The origins of Freemasonry are obscure. Masonic historians claim various pedigrees for their craft, with some seeking direct descent from the mythical architect of Solomon's Temple, Hiram Abif, himself. As Judaism prohibits the making of graven images, architecture was the one discipline in which the Divine could be represented. As St Bernard wrote, God is 'length, width, height and depth', and tradition holds that Solomon's Temple not only represented Divinity, but actually embodied it; God was literally present in the building, both within its space and also its very fabric. The Templars were thought to have discovered the secrets of Solomon's Temple (while excavating under the Temple Mount, one presumes), and also had their own stonemasons. The Templars were known to have been avid builders and, as we have seen, some suggest that Templar masons even played a part in introducing Gothic architecture into Europe. In this way, the Order acted as a bridge between the original Temple builders in Jerusalem and the various strands of Freemasonry that emerged during the seventeenth century.

The earliest precise date we have for Freemasonry is Sir

Robert Moray's initiation into a lodge in Newcastle on 20 May 1641, with Elias Ashmole recording his own initiation five years later. The Grand Lodge of England was founded in 1717, with the eighteenth century marking the official public emergence of Freemasonry. Initially, the Masonic movement didn't publicly lay claim to a Templar pedigree, although that would soon change. In 1736, one Andrew Michael Ramsay delivered a speech, known as Ramsay's Oration, in which he attempted to sell Masonry to the power behind the French throne, Cardinal Fleury. Ramsay claimed that Masonry was essentially an ancient mystery tradition that had reached the West via 'the Crusaders', although he did not mention the Templars by name. However, given the importance of Solomon's Temple in Masonic legend, it was only a matter of time before the Templars were being invoked as Masonic forebears, with the Templars themselves in no position to counter the claims.

Perhaps the most notable of the early Templarist Masons was the German noble Baron Karl Gottlieb von Hund, who claimed to have been initiated into Freemasonry in Paris by an 'unknown superior'. This form of Freemasonry was known as the Strict Templar Observance and Hund became its chief propagator. Hund claimed that this form of Masonry derived directly from the Knights Templar themselves; indeed, at the highest degree of initiation in Strict Templar Observance Masonry one became a 'Knight Templar'. But Hund was not alone in promulgating Masonic Templarism. He had rivals and successors in the shape of a German pastor by the name of Samuel Rosa, a somewhat dubious Scot who called himself George Frederick Johnson and Johann August Starck – to name but three – all of whom started their own Masonic traditions and all of which claimed to be derived from the Templars.

As we noted earlier, Templarist groups were even thought to

have played a part in the French Revolution and enthusiasm for all things Templar continued into the Napoleonic era, with even Napoleon himself becoming obsessed with the Order. During the early nineteenth century, a Frenchman called Bernard Raymond Fabré-Palaprat, who founded a Masonic order called the Sovereign Military Order of the Temple of Jerusalem, claimed to have discovered a document that showed all the Templar Grand Masters *since* de Molay, beginning with Jean-Marc Larmenius, who supposedly took over in 1314. Fabré-Palaprat claimed that this so-called 'Larmenius Charter' was in fact at least 100 years old and that he himself was the latest 'official' Templar Grand Master, as opposed to all the other traditions that were claiming Templar descent. Although Fabré-Palaprat's claims are, in the main, not taken seriously, the Templars continue to enjoy a prestigious reputation in modern Masonry – for example, like Hund's Strict Templar Observance, York Rite Masonry has the Knight Templar as its highest degree – but no incontrovertible evidence has yet come to light definitively linking Freemasonry with the mediaeval Templars.

The Templar *Ordensland*

Unlike the Teutonic Knights and the Hospitallers, the Templars never managed to create their own *Ordensland*, or state. (Prussia in the case of the Teutonic Knights, while the Hospitallers established themselves on Rhodes and later Malta.) The Languedoc – where support for the Order was particularly strong – and Cyprus would have been the most likely locations for a Templar state, such a move offering protection from both Philip and the Pope. After 1312, former Templars found sanctuary in Spain and Portugal, while other countries have also been mooted as possible Templar havens.

Scotland, as we have noted, has been championed by various writers as being one of the locations fugitive Templars could have fled to after the suppression of the Order. At odds with both England and the Papacy, Scotland could certainly have offered a safe haven and in a charter from 1488, King James IV of Scotland reaffirmed the Templars' traditional rights and privileges, suggesting 'that as late as the fifteenth century the Scottish Templars had some kind of legal existence.'[64] What became of the Scottish Templars after this date remains unclear, but a number of theories suggest Templar survival in the form of chivalric orders such as the Scots Guard or in Freemasonry.

Another haven for fleeing Templars could have been provided by the then emerging country of Switzerland. One theory has been put forward[65] that a group of Templars became involved with the struggle for Swiss independence some time after the first three Cantons – Uri, Schwyz and Unterwalden – signed a pact of mutual assistance in 1291. Swiss folk tales tell of white-clad knights appearing to assist the Cantons in the struggle against the Holy Roman Empire; the date is also significant, as, after 1291, the Templars were seemingly without a *raison d'être* for their continued existence. Whether or not these knights – assuming they were Templars – saw the emerging Swiss confederacy as a potential *Ordensland* of their own is impossible now to determine, but two factors lend credibility to this thesis: firstly, the Swiss, once established, suddenly acquired, as if from nowhere, the best army in Europe. Their military prowess would remain unchallenged until the Battle of Marignano in 1515, when they were comprehensively defeated by the French. Secondly, Switzerland is famous (or infamous, depending upon one's point of view) for its banks. The Templars were the true originators of the international banking system that is still in use today, predating the great Italian houses by more than a century.

Perhaps it is this that is the Templars main legacy to us. As Desmond Seward notes, 'no medieval institution did more for the rise of capitalism'[66] than the Templars.

Umberto Eco joked in his novel *Foucault's Pendulum*, a send-up of the conspiracy theory view of history, that 'the Templars have something to do with everything'.[67] But if Seward's contention is correct, the Templars could indeed be said to 'have something to do with everything', in the sense that the modern world has been profoundly moulded by the values and beliefs that emerged during the High Middle Ages, the period in which the Templars flourished and on which they exercised such an enormous influence. Likewise, if the Order did indeed pave the way for modern capitalism, its ghost is still very much with us.[68] In that sense, the Templar *Ordensland* was not created in space, but in time: it is an era that was ushered in with the Enlightenment in the eighteenth century and, for better or worse, persists to this day.

A Fable Agreed Upon?

In order to appreciate fully the Templars, both as an historical phenomenon and as the white-mantled knights who have ridden across the pages of writers from Guillaume of Tyre's chronicles to Walter Scott's *Ivanhoe* and Dan Brown's *The Da Vinci Code*, we have to understand that the Templars are as much a product of myth as they are of history. Such, however, are the strengths of both myth and history that it sometimes appears that each writer who deals with them is seemingly writing about a different Order, from the academics who maintain that they were, in reality, very ordinary men, to the more speculative camp who portray the Templars as a secret society of mystical initiates.

Myth has surrounded the Order since its inception. St Bernard of Clairvaux himself, while being their earliest apologist, was also their first mythologiser, portraying them as 'gentler than lambs and more ferocious than lions'. Even the Templars themselves – or at least rank and file members – seem to have believed their own myths: during the trial, Templar brothers were questioned about the origins of the Order. Their answers are instructive: they were generally hazy about when – and indeed precisely why – the Order began. They tended to accept as fact the story that the Order was indeed founded by nine knights who were so poor they didn't even have enough money for equipment or horses; the Templars' famous seal – showing two knights riding the same horse – was proof if any were needed. And of course myth has shrouded the end of the Order as well: Dante felt that the Templars were innocent, but his contemporary, the Majorcan mystic Ramon Lull, who had personally met Jacques de Molay, believed that they were guilty as charged, while – perhaps somewhat oddly – the great inquisitor Bernard Gui couldn't decide what to make of charges against the Order.

Rumours and opinion about the Order 'fluctuated rather aimlessly'[69] for more than two centuries until the great Renaissance scholar and magus Cornelius Agrippa wrote in his *De occulta philosophia* (written around 1510, but not published until 1531) that the Templars had committed 'detestable heresy'.[70] Agrippa's massive book was the most influential of all Renaissance magical texts and his comments effected a sea-change in how the Order was perceived. From then on, they were either heroes or villains, depending upon one's view of heretics (Agrippa equates the Order with witchcraft). For the political theorist Jean Bodin (1530–96), who loathed Agrippa, the Templars were unjustly persecuted and he compares their plight with that of other persecuted minorities, including the Jews, the Gnostics and Christians in the Roman Empire. This polarisation continued into the seventeenth century. The official French historians Pierre and Jacques Dupuy wrote in defence of Philip and published original trial documents in 1654 to back up their claims, while the English antiquarian Elias Ashmole described the Templars in his history of the Order of the Garter (who looked to the Templars for inspiration) as 'a noble Order, no less famous for martial achievements in the east, than their wealthy possessions in the west... Which gave occasion to many sober men to judge, that their wealth was their greatest crime'.[71] And in the eighteenth and nineteenth centuries, as we have seen, the Templars were championed by the various competing forms of Masonic Templarism and later by the great occult revival of the nineteenth century. By the twentieth century, the Templars only seemed to be vaguely visible through the haze of myth and rumour surrounding them.

As Michael Baigent and Richard Leigh point out,[72] the two basic schools of thought concerning the Templars – the academic and the mythic – tend to remain firmly apart. On the one hand, academic historians will only consider whether something 'actually happened' when it can be backed up by documentation and other forms of evidence, whereas the more speculative apologists for the Order thrive on the myths and legends surrounding them. Baigent and Leigh argue that something does not need to have 'actually happened' in order for it to become subsumed into the collective consciousness and affect later generations. Myths themselves are historical 'facts' in the sense that they have been present in recorded history and have had varying degrees of influence. The Grail Romances, for instance, were enormously popular from their first appearance and played a part in shaping mediaeval notions of knighthood and chivalry. For a more modern myth that has had an effect on history, one need look no further than the myth of Aryan supremacy, which the Nazis held to be gospel with such appallingly catastrophic results.

Where the Templars are concerned, there is a huge dichotomy between the orthodox history and the myth and it can only be possible to understand the Order as a whole if the mythical aspect is also considered alongside the facts. Umberto Eco points out[73] that the conspiracy theorists tend to project a great deal of their own failings into their theories, no matter how wild. What he does not mention, however, is that the hands that write the more standard, orthodox history can also be driven by similar forces: the desire for peer acceptance, the desire to maintain one's position within academe and, perhaps more importantly, one's funding, all of which would be severely compromised by entertaining the more mythical – or even the less historically verifiable – aspects of the Templar story. Emerson's dictum that history needs to be written 'broader and deeper' is advice that Templar writers would do well to heed, but, so far, very few have treated the Order in this interdisciplinary way.[74]

Why should myths, stories, half-truths and theories – whether about the Templars and their alleged activities or more modern variants such as UFOs, or who shot President Kennedy – appeal to us, even remain somehow vital? Karen Armstrong writes that 'human beings have always been mythmakers'.[75] A myth is valid 'if it forces us to change our minds and hearts, gives us new hope, and compels us to live more fully'.[76] Perhaps it is also because we are children of two worlds: that of recorded and recordable history, and also that of the imagination. Indeed, what we think plays an enormous role in actually shaping the world we encounter and live in. In a culture that prides itself on secular materialism, specialisation is encouraged; professors of myth and history do not venture into the other's field, books on the Templars are either one or the other, the twain never meeting, and our two ways of making sense of the world – the historical and the mythic – are kept apart. But this is not our daily experience of our lives, where the two worlds constantly overlap and blend. We need both history and myth, otherwise we are getting only half the story, not just about the world, but also, in some way, about ourselves. And, it should be remembered, the act of making sense of both the world and ourselves happens within our own imaginations and within the unchanging present moment of our own awareness; therefore history as much as myth could be said to be timeless, because it can only happen within our awareness. In the realm of the imagination, therefore, history and myth could be said to be still happening, over and over, which gives both a continuing relevance. In this sense, it would therefore be possible to see the Templars as both ordinary soldier-monks and as mystical initiates operating behind the scenes if we are able to appreciate the truths of both versions of the story, the truths that recorded history informs us of, and the deeper, more elusive stratas of truth that myths give us. In this way, the myths and stories about the Templars could indeed '[compel] us to live more fully'.

The great Tibetan saint Padmasambhava's dictum, 'Things are not what they seem; nor are they otherwise', aptly describes the apparent paradoxes of the Templars and the myths surrounding them. That the Order was fanatically secretive forever compounds the difficulty of arriving at anything close to a definitive account, but if that account is ever to appear, it would likely have to argue that the Templars were, in the main, very ordinary men, but that certain elements of the Order could indeed have been 'tainted' with heterodox thinking. Whether we will ever know with what, is, of course, another matter and whether recent discoveries such as the Chinon Parchment force us to re-evaluate our thinking about the Templars, one thing remains certain: the mystique and fascination of the Order of Poor Knights of Christ and the Temple of Solomon will continue to exert its hold and the aura surrounding the Order will continue, maybe deepen even further, and perhaps never be fully fathomed. The mystery will remain.

Afterword: Parchment, Grail and Shroud

The Chinon Parchment

The discovery of the Chinon Parchment in the Vatican secret archives is the single most important Templar discovery in decades and throws considerable new light on the Order's demise. The document is the record of the interrogations of the Templar leadership at Chinon castle in August 1308, conducted by the Pope's agents. After being incorrectly archived in the seventeenth century, it lay undisturbed until it was unearthed by Dr Barbara Frale in 2001.

The parchment confirms that the Templars did indeed spit on the cross and deny Christ during their initiation ceremony, apparently to test the obedience of the new recruit (for the full list of charges, see Appendix III). It was not unusual for the military orders to develop their own rituals and, given the Templars' untouchable position for much of their existence, it is perhaps not surprising that they developed rituals of their own.

But why spitting on the cross and denying Christ? Such things have played into the hands of conspiracy theorists, who have seen this as evidence that the Templars were heretics, but it seems the ritual evolved from the testimony of early Templar escapees from Muslim jails, who had been forced to do such things while in captivity. Spitting on the cross, therefore, was simply a way of testing the new recruit's mettle. Similarly, as Barbara Frale has argued, the charge of sodomy was derived from a misunderstanding of the new recruit being encouraged to relieve his physical desires with other brothers, rather than with a woman. This was not, as the French prosecution alleged, a sign of institutional homosexuality, but was another test for the would-be Templar. If he could do as his superior instructed him during the initiation ceremony, he was seen as suitable material and was admitted to the Order. These explanations satisfied Clement, who declared the Order to be not guilty of heresy, and reconciled the Templars to the Church.

But the Chinon Parchment does not explain why de Molay and the other Templar leaders took back their retractions in front of Clement's cardinals. The whole purpose of the Chinon hearings was to get the truth from the Templar leadership without the 'aid' of torture; de Molay and his colleagues were therefore encouraged to tell Clement's men the whole truth, rather than what Philip and de Nogaret wanted to hear. Yet they went back to their original confessions of the previous autumn, which had been extracted under torture. No satisfactory explanation for this bizarre behaviour has been put forward. We can only assume it was a combination of stress, fear and political misjudgement, but we cannot be certain, unless further documents come to light.

Chinon was also the nearest Jacques de Molay ever came to meeting the Pope himself, who was several miles away at the time of the questioning, but never personally visited the castle. De Molay claimed he could save the Order if he could only meet Clement in person. But again, this didn't happen. Philip must have known about this and made sure the two men never met. One wonders what de Molay would have said had Clement been at Chinon in person.

The Holy Grail

Despite the revelations of the Chinon Parchment, a number of other questions remain. Among them, we might note a mysterious rite 'unknown to the Roman Church'[77] that the Templars performed on Holy (Maundy) Thursday. The ceremony was held to commemorate the Last Supper, in which the Templars received communion in the form of wine only – no bread. Quite where this ritual came from is a mystery, although Barbara Frale suggests that the Templars 'seem to have borrowed it from certain ancient popular religious traditions practised in the city of Jerusalem, perhaps as far back as the early Christian era'.[78] This is itself interesting, as it implies that the Templars discovered a secret Christian tradition alive and well in Jerusalem, one that did not filter back to Europe. Frale also sees a link between the Holy Thursday rite and the Holy Grail, which the Templars were said to be guardians of. Does this then suggest that the legends surrounding the Templars and the Grail might have some truth in them? Without further evidence, the rite – unique to the Templars – remains a puzzle.

Frale suggests a further link with the Grail. She notes that many churches in Constantinople possessed reliquaries that were claimed to contain droplets of Christ's blood. After the city was sacked by Crusaders in 1204, many of these reliquaries found their way back to Europe, where they may have influenced the growing legend of the Grail. No longer was the Grail a Christianised version of the Celtic Cauldron of Plenty: the cup used at the Last Supper was now also the cup that Joseph of Arimathea caught drops of the Holy Blood in on Calvary. And where could the reliquaries have acquired the Holy Blood from in the first place? From bloodstains – the so-called 'Belt of Blood' – on the Mandylion, or Holy Shroud, which had been kept in the Imperial Collection but, like the reliquaries and countless other relics, disappeared after 1204. The Mandylion, Frale believes, is nothing other than the Turin Shroud.

The Turin Shroud

The records of the trial of the Templars in Carcassonne had never been fully translated before Barbara Frale examined them. To her surprise, she read how one Arnaut Sabbatier, who joined the Order in 1287, testified after the arrests that, during his initiation he was taken to 'a secret place to which only the brothers of the Temple had access' and was shown 'a long linen cloth on which was impressed the figure of a man'. Sabbatier was instructed to venerate the image by kissing its feet three times.[79] Was this the Shroud of Turin? Frale believes so. The fact that the image shown to Sabbatier was of an entire body seems to preclude it being one of the other so-called Holy Faces – relics such as the Veronica, or the Keramion – which are miraculously imprinted with the face (but not the body) of Christ. Ian Wilson has argued that the Shroud had been looted from Constantinople in 1204 when Crusaders sacked the city. This would account for the 'gap' in the Shroud's history, when it seems to disappear from view, not resurfacing until the display of the Shroud at Lirey in 1357.[80]

Barbara Frale believes this theory to be highly probable. She argues that, after being removed from Constantinople, the Shroud passed into the custody of the French noble Othon de La Roche, who hid the Shroud on his estates near Athens. When the Latin Empire of Constantinople collapsed in 1261, the Shroud then passed to the Templars by way of one of Othon's descendants, Amaury de La Roche, who was commander of the Templars in the East, and also a member of the inner circle – a *compaignon* – of the Grand Master, Thomas Bérard. The Shroud seems to have been kept in various Templar castles, but after the fall of Safad in 1266, it was decided to bring the Shroud to the West, where it was moved between various Templar preceptories in France, Provence in particular.

Frale notes that, during the Trial, many accounts of the Templar idol came from Provence, and she believes a 'cult of the Shroud' started in the 1260s, under the auspices of the Preceptor of Provence, Roncelin de Fos. From this time on, the linen belts the Templars wore no longer symbolised chastity and purity, but represented their link to Christ, having been consecrated by contact with the Shroud. With Jerusalem long lost and the Holy Land being ravaged by Baybars, the actual burial shroud of Christ was, for the Templars, almost a 'new sepulchre', a relic capable of conveying Christ's earthly existence like no other. This would have been particularly useful in Provence, where there seem to have been more heretical Templars than anywhere else. Many were Cathars who had joined the Order to escape the Albigensian Crusade and, later, the Inquisition, which had been set up in 1231 with the sole intention of rooting out Catharism. The Cathars were docetists – that is, they believed Christ did not really have a corporeal body, but was a kind of divine spirit, and that he did not suffer on the cross. The Shroud was proof against this: it showed Christ's wounds, his suffering, his death, all too clearly.

With the Cult of the Shroud established, copies of the face were made and distributed among Templar houses all over the West – the Templecombe panel in England being one such copy. But the Shroud was kept secret, only unveiled at certain times, to certain people. The decision to keep the Shroud secret was, Frale believes, a necessity, as admitting to possessing it would have resulted in excommunication, the penalty meted out to anyone owning relics stolen from Constantinople. But this decision was also a tragic mistake – as it led to the accusations of idolatry, devil worship and sorcery that surfaced during the trial.

Although Frale does not speculate on why de Molay and

other leading Templars kept quiet about the Shroud during the Trial, we can assume that the cult of secrecy was so strong that de Molay could not admit to the Order's possessing it even then, or only planned to if he had ever had the chance of a face to face meeting with Clement. Then again, perhaps it was simply a matter of keeping their most prized relic out of the hands of Philip the Fair. Once the Order was suppressed, we can assume the Shroud remained in Templar hands, with the de Charney family, who were the first to display it, at Lirey in 1357.

If Frale's corroboration of Ian Wilson's theory is correct, it paints the Templars not as heretics, but as devoutly Christian; almost desperately so, in the sense that the Shroud was the last link with the lost kingdom of the Christian East, a tangible reminder of Christ's presence on Earth, symbolised by the haunting, literally tortured features of the Man of Sorrows. Viewed from the standpoint of esoteric Christianity, the Shroud also fits the description of the Baphomet as symbolising the Completed Man, in the sense that Christ is the Father of Understanding and the embodiment of Wisdom.[81]

*

There are further mysteries still: why, for instance, did the Templars revere Mary Magdalene and John the Baptist above all other saints (the Virgin Mary excepted)? Were they aware of the belief – held by the Cathars of the Languedoc – that the Magdalene was the wife of Christ, while John, according to the Mandaeans, was the true Messiah?

And why does a French Templar seal, from the early thirteenth century, feature the Gnostic god Abraxas?

Just when it seems we can safely consign the Templars to history, the myths and mysteries reappear to keep their history shifting, elusive and alive.

Endnotes

[1] Baigent, Leigh & Lincoln, *The Holy Blood and the Holy Grail* (Jonathan Cape, 1982), p.51.

[2] Genesis 22:12–18.

[3] Daniel, 'The Life and Journey of Daniel', in *Jerusalem Pilgrimage*, ed. J Wilkinson, Hakluyt Society 167 (London, 1988). Quoted in Barber, *The New Knighthood* (Cambridge University Press, 1994), p.3.

[4] Daniel, *ibid*. Quoted in Barber, *op. cit.*, p.6.

[5] St Bernard, from a letter to Pope Calixtus II, 1124/5. Quoted in Barber, *op. cit.*, p.13.

[6] All of these knights were among the original nine members. According to Barber (*op. cit.*, p.12), King Baldwin had already sent two of the original nine Templars, André de Montbard and Gondemar, to France for Church approval of the Order. This would leave only the unknown ninth member (Hugh of Champagne?) in Outremer, reinforcing the theory that the Templars – in order to be taken seriously by Baldwin II, the Pope and the Council of Troyes – had to be more than nine knights strong by 1129.

[7] Guigo, Lettres des Premiers Chartreux, *Sources Chrétiennes* 88, Paris 1988. Quoted in Barber, *op. cit.*, p.49.

[8] Barber, *op. cit.*, p.42.

[9] Quoted in Read, *The Templars* (Weidenfeld & Nicholson, 1999), p.119.

[10] Barber, *op. cit.*, p.230.

[11] RC Smail, *Crusading Warfare, 1097–1193* (Cambridge, 1995), p.43.

[12] Theodericus, ch.17, pp.26–7 in *Jerusalem Pilgrimage*, pp.293–4; quoted in Barber, *op. cit.* pp.90–93.

[13] Genesis 32:24–29.

[14] Read, *op. cit.*, p.155.

[15] Read, *ibid.*, p.158.

[16] Quoted in Barber, *op. cit.,* p.115.

[17] Barber, *ibid.*, p.116.

ENDNOTES

18 Gestes des Chiprois, pp.252–3; quoted in Barber, *op. cit.*, pp.241–3.

19 Seward, *The Monks of War* (Penguin Books, 1992), p.37.

20 The connection between Lazarus and leprosy is a mysterious one. Lazarus, in John's Gospel, did not suffer from the disease. The Order of Lazarus may have, however, taken its name from a lesser-known Lazarus who appears in Luke 16.19–31, and who was said to have been covered in sores. It is possible that the Templars used Lazar houses for purposes other than that of treating lepers, knowing that fear of the disease would mean that the houses would remain undisturbed.

21 Barber, *op. cit.*, p.64.

22 For a treatment of children raised in silence, see John Burnside's novel *The Dumb House* (Cape, 1997); for the search for the language of Eden, see Umberto Eco's *The Search for the Perfect Language* (Blackwell, 1997).

23 Some chronologies list Richard de Bures as the Grand Master between Armand and Guillaume. As no list of Grand Masters is definitive, we can assume that either Richard actually was the head of the Order between La Forbie and Guillaume de Sonnac's election in c.1247, or that he was acting as a caretaker Grand Master who would have stepped aside had Armand de Périgord emerged from captivity or until a successor could officially replace him.

24 Barber, *op. cit.*, p.152.

25 Quoted in Read, *op. cit.*, p.228.

26 *Flores Historiarum* (London, 1890); quoted in Barber, *op. cit.*, p.157.

27 Although the Fall of Acre is usually seen as the end of the Christian presence in the East, there was one remaining Christian stronghold in the Holy Land after 1291, the Templar castle of La Roche Guillaume, in the Amanus March, which held out against all odds until 1299. See Malcolm Barber and Keith Bate, *The Templars: Selected Sources* (MUP, 2002), p.15.

28 Barber, *The Trial of the Templars* (Cambridge University Press, 1978), p.48.

29 A result of de Nogaret's attempts to kidnap Boniface VIII at Agnani in September 1303.

30 Quoted in Read, *op. cit.*, p.265.

31 Quoted in Read, *op. cit.*, p.295.

32 Edward Burman, *Supremely Abominable Crimes* (Allison & Busby, 1994), p.266.

33 Burman, *ibid.*, p.272.

34 The fate of de Molay's and de Charney's remains is a mystery, although Phil Rickman suggests a possible last resting place for the Grand Master in his novel *The Fabric of Sin*.

[35] Sir Steven Runciman, *A History of the Crusades*, Vol. III (Penguin, 1990–1), pp.435–6. Charges of heresy were also brought against the Hospitallers, in 1238, and the Teutonic Knights, in 1307.

[36] Runciman, *ibid*, Vol. II, p.477.

[37] Hugh was not known as 'de Payens' until 1125 at the earliest. See Karen Ralls, *The Templars and the Grail* (Quest Books, 2003), pp.36–7. Some scholars have speculated that his original name was 'de Pagens', and 'Paganus' is presumably a garbling of this, although, given the number of theories suggesting that the Templars were in some way heretical, is Walter suggesting that Hugh de Payen was in some sense a pagan?

[38] Baigent, Leigh & Lincoln, *op. cit.*, p.57.

[39] Barber, *The New Knighthood*, p.8.

[40] Helen Nicholson, *The Knights Templar: A New History* (Sutton, 2001), pp.29–30.

[41] Barber & Bate, *op. cit.*, p.2.

[42] e.g. Baigent, Leigh & Lincoln, *op. cit.*, pp.35–65, pp.81–100, in particular pp.62–5.

[43] The mediaeval Order of Sion has nothing whatsoever to do with the modern 'Priory of Sion', which is largely a hoax dreamed up by French fascists. For more on their bizarre story, see Lynn Picknett and Clive Prince's *The Sion Revelation* (Little, Brown, 2006).

[44] The phrase was coined by Templar researchers Stephen Dafoe and Alan Butler. See their *Templar Continuum* (Templar Books, 1999).

[45] NH Mazet, *Daggers*, Part I: The Templars, p.18 (eBook, 2001).

[46] Legends of tunnels beneath Templar properties are legion. They were probably a means of escape in most cases.

[47] Barbara Frale, *The Templars: The Secret History Revealed*, p.202.

[48] Ralls, *op. cit.*, p.130.

[49] Baigent, Leigh & Lincoln, *op. cit.*, p.67.

[50] Baigent, Leigh & Lincoln, *op. cit.*, pp.67–8.

[51] Karen Ralls, *op. cit.*, p.66. Ralls also notes (p.3) that the enigmatic graffiti carved in the dungeons of Chinon Castle by imprisoned Templars in 1308 is suggestive that they were privy to an esoteric tradition. Likewise, the Order was thought to have been responsible for the dissemination in Europe of Tarot cards, thought by some to embody arcane wisdom.

[52] Speculative researchers might see this changing of patron saints – from the Almoner to the Baptist – as proof that the Hospitallers were also secret Mandaeans or Johannites. They were, after all, accused of heresy in 1238, decades before the downfall of the Templars...

ENDNOTES

53 'Vatican File Shows Pope Pardoned Massacred Knights', *The Times*, 30 March 2002.

54 Idries Shah, *The Sufis* (Octagon Press, 1964), p.226.

55 See, for instance, Keith Laidler, *The Divine Deception* (Headline, 2000) and Christopher Knight and Robert Lomas, *The Second Messiah* (Random House, 1997). Both of these books suggest that the Templars actually *created* the Shroud, the face on it either being that of Jesus (as the Man of Sorrows?) or Jacques de Molay.

56 Frale, *op. cit*, p.175.

57 In addition to London, there are intact round churches in Cambridge – not definitely Templar, being apparently built by the mysterious Order of the Holy Sepulchre, but certainly twelfth century – and a Hospitaller round church at Little Maplestead in Essex. Foundations of round churches can also be seen at the Templar preceptories of Garway, Temple Bruer and Dover.

58 A further enigma of Templar churches, regardless of shape, is that they are not aligned directly on an east–west axis, as is normal practice. Simon Brighton suggests that the churches, at least in England, were aligned according to patronal principles. That is to say, they were aligned towards the spot on the horizon where the sun rose on the feast day of the saint to which the church or building was dedicated, while the Templar chapel at Moffat in Dumfries and Galloway seems to have been aligned towards the west. See Brighton, p.242 and pp.230–1.

59 William and Henry's family name has various spellings: St Clair, Sinclair, St Clare, St Cleer and Saintclaire. Sinclair tends to be the more popular variant today.

60 Quoted in Mark Hedsel, *The Zelator* (Random House, 1998), p.131.

61 Michael Baigent & Richard Leigh, *The Temple and the Lodge* (Cape, 1989), p.84.

62 See Ralls, *op. cit.*, pp. 26–7.

63 Baigent & Leigh, *op. cit.*, p.88.

64 Ralls, *op. cit.*, p.114.

65 Alan Butler & Stephen Dafoe, *The Warriors and the Bankers* (Templar Books, 1998).

66 Seward, *op. cit.*, p.222.

67 Umberto Eco, *Foucault's Pendulum* (Secker & Warburg, 1989), p.375.

68 The Templars are also 'still with us' in the sense that the Knights of Christ – the Portuguese Order founded for Templar survivors after de Molay's execution – still exists, although it is now a ceremonial order, into which

ENDNOTES

one is usually inducted as a sign of honour in Portugal. The Templars' great rivals, the Hospitallers, also continue to exist as the Knights of Malta, while the Teutonic Knights continue to exist as the German Order.

69 Quoted in Peter Partner, *The Murdered Magicians* (Oxford University Press, 1981), p.90.

70 Partner, *op. cit.*, p.92. Agrippa was not the only occultist to study the Templars. In 1910, Aleister Crowley was admitted to the OTO, or *Ordo Templi Orientis* – the Order of Oriental Templars. Emerging out of late 19th-century freemasonry, the OTO under Crowley became decidedly more esoteric in its practices, arguably becoming one of the most influential bodies in 20th-century ritual magic.

71 Elias Ashmole, *Institutions, Laws and Ceremonies of the Most Noble Order of the Garter* (1672). Quoted in Partner, *op. cit.*, p.97.

72 Baigent & Leigh, *op. cit.*, pp.127–31.

73 *Foucault's Pendulum*, p.619.

74 One of the few writers to have done so to date is Dr Karen Ralls, whose book *The Templars and the Grail* surveys both the orthodox and speculative accounts of the Templar story.

75 Karen Armstrong, *A Short History of Myth* (Canongate, 2005), p.1.

76 Armstrong, *op. cit.*, p.10.

77 Frale, p. 201.

78 Frale, p. 201.

79 'Knights Templar hid the Shroud of Turin, says Vatican', *The Times*, 6 April, 2009.

80 For more on the various Faces and shrouds, see Ian Wilson's *Holy Faces, Secret Places* (Transworld, 1991).

81 Of course, none of this brings us any closer to understanding what the Shroud actually *is*. The 1988 radiocarbon dating remains controversial, with believers demanding that another sample of cloth be dated as they claim that the original sample used was actually from a mediaeval repair to the Shroud. For non-believers, amongst the most interesting theories about the Shroud are those that claim it's the world's first photograph, created with a camera obscura and a fixing solution made using natural ingredients that would have been available to a mediaeval 'photographer' (quite possibly an alchemist). A number of new 'Shrouds' have been created this way. See the work of South African scholar Dr Nicholas P Allen, amongst others, for further details.

82 Baigent, Leigh & Lincoln, *op. cit.*, chapter 5.

Appendix I:
Chronology

1168	Templars refuse to participate in the Egyptian campaign
1173	Assassin envoy murdered by the Templars
1187 (1 May)	Battle of the Springs of Cresson
(4 July)	Battle of Hattin
(2 October)	Jerusalem falls to Saladin
1188	Council of Gisors: the 'Cutting of the Elm'
1189–92	The Third Crusade
1192	Templars move headquarters to Acre
1191–92	Templars occupy – and for a short time, own – Cyprus
1191–1216	Templars and Leo of Armenia in conflict over the Amanus March
1198	Foundation of the Teutonic Knights
1202–04	The Fourth Crusade
1208	Innocent III accuses the Templars of necromancy; Start of the Albigensian Crusade
1217–21	Building of the castle of 'Atlit (Pilgrim's Castle)
1218–21	The Fifth Crusade
1228–29	The Sixth Crusade
1239–40	Crusade of Theobald of Champagne
1240–41	Crusade of Richard of Cornwall
1240	Rebuilding of Safad begins
1241–42	Siege of the Hospital compound at Acre
1243	Eviction of Imperial forces from Tyre
1244 (16 March)	Fall of Cathar stronghold at Montségur
(23 August)	Loss of Jerusalem
(17 October)	Battle of La Forbie
1248–54	The Seventh Crusade
1250 (8 February)	Battle of Mansurah
1257–67	Additional clauses on penances added to the Rule
1266	Fall of Safad to the Mamluks
After 1268	Catalan Rule of the Templars
1271–72	Crusade of Edward of England – truce negotiated with Mamluks
1274	Council of Lyon
1277	Maria of Antioch sells her rights to the throne of Jerusalem to Charles of Anjou
1277–82	Civil War in Tripoli
1291 (May)	Fall of Acre to the Mamluks

1291 (August)	Templars evacuate Tortosa and 'Atlit
1299	Fall of La Roche Guillaume
1300	Templars attack Egyptian coastal towns
1300–01	Abortive attempt to retake the Holy Land
1302	Loss of Ruad and massacre of the Templar garrison
1305	First allegations made against the Order by Esquin de Floyran
1306	Templars support Amaury in coup in Cyprus; Jacques de Molay returns to the West
1307 (13 October)	Arrest of the Templars in France
(19 October)	Parisian hearings begin
(24 October)	Jacques de Molay's first confession
(22 November)	*Pastoralis praeeminentiae* calls for Templars everywhere to be arrested
(24 December)	De Molay retracts his confession before Papal committee
1308 (February)	Clement suspends proceedings
(27 June)	72 Templars confess before Clement
(August)	Papal Commissions launched; De Molay interviewed at Chinon, retracts his retraction
1309 (22 November)	Papal commission begins its proceedings
(26 & 28 November)	De Molay appears before commission
1310 (April)	Templar defence begins
(12 May)	Burning of 54 Templars as relapsed heretics near Paris
1311 (5 June)	Papal hearings finally end
(16 October)	Council of Vienne begins
1312 (22 March)	*Vox in excelso* abolishes the Temple
(2 May)	*Ad providam* transfers Temple property to the Hospital
(6 May)	*Considerantes dudum* allows provincial councils to judge cases
1314 (18 March)	Burning of Jacques de Molay and Geoffroi de Charney
(20 April)	Pope Clement V dies
(24 June)	Battle of Bannockburn
(29 November)	Philip the Fair dies
1319	*Ad ea exquibis* recognises the Knights of Christ
1571	Presumed destruction of the Templar archive on Cyprus by the Ottomans

Appendix II:
Grand Masters of the Temple

There is no definitive list of Templar Grand Masters. If one ever existed, then it is possible that it was amongst the documents destroyed by Jacques de Molay shortly before the arrests of 1307 or it could have vanished along with the rest of the Templar archive, the fate of which remains an unsolved mystery. The earliest known list dates from 1342.

c.1119–c.1136	Hugues de Payen
c.1136–c.1149	Robert de Craon
c.1149–c.1152	Everard des Barres*
c.1152–1153	Bernard de Tremelay
1153–1156	André de Montbard*
1156–1169	Bertrand de Blancfort
1169–1171	Philip de Nablus*
c.1171–1179	Odo de St Amand
1181–1184	Arnold of Torroja
1185–1189	Gerard de Ridefort
1191–1192/3	Robert de Sablé
1194–1200	Gilbert Erail
1201–1209	Philip de Plessis
1210–1218/19	Guillaume de Chartres
1219–1230/32	Peter de Montaigu
c.1232–1244	Armand de Périgord
c.1244–c.1247	Richard de Bures*
c.1247–1250	Guillaume de Sonnac
1250–1256	Reginald de Vichiers
1256–1273	Thomas Bérard
1273–1291	Guillaume de Beaujeu
1291–1292/93	Theobald Gaudin
c.1293–1314	Jacques de Molay

*Disputed.

Many Grand Master lists omit Richard de Bures (see Note 23, page 156).

The Masterships of Everard des Barres and André de Montbard have been called into question by Baigent, Leigh and Lincoln in *The Holy Blood and the Holy Grail*.[82] As regional masters and Grand Masters often signed themselves as '*magister templi*', it has often led to confusion about precisely who was Grand Master and who was merely a regional master.

All the Masters died in office, with the exception of Everard des Barres, who resigned to become a monk at Clairvaux, where he was still living in 1176, and Philip de Nablus, who apparently also resigned. While Hugues de Payen died in his bed, other Masters were not so lucky: Bernard de Tremelay died during the siege of Ascalon; Gerard de Ridefort at Acre; Guillaume de Sonnac at Mansurah; Guillaume de Beaujeu during the Fall of Acre; Jacques de Molay was executed as a relapsed heretic. Odo de St Amand and Armand de Périgord both died in Muslim jails.

Gilbert Erail was the only Grand Master to be excommunicated (later rescinded by Pope Innocent III).

In the nineteenth century, a Masonic document surfaced claiming to list all the Grand Masters of the now-underground Templar movement, starting with Jean-Marc Larmenius, who is alleged to have taken over from Jacques de Molay in 1314. It is generally regarded as extremely spurious, and is not quoted here.

Appendix III:
The Charges Against the Templars

Although by June 1308 127 charges had been made against the Templars, the initial charges of the previous October fall into these nine basic categories:

1. That during the reception ceremony, new brothers were required to deny Christ, God, the Virgin or the Saints on the command of those receiving them.
2. That the brothers committed various sacrilegious acts – trampling, spitting, urinating – either on the Cross or on an image of Christ.
3. That the receptors practised obscene kisses on new entrants, on the mouth, navel, base of the spine or buttocks.
4. That Templar priests did not consecrate the host, and that the brothers did not believe in the sacraments.
5. That the brothers practised idol worship of a cat or a head, called Baphomet.
6. That the brothers practised institutional sodomy.
7. That the Grand Master, or other high-ranking officials, absolved fellow Templars of their sins.
8. That the Templars held their reception ceremonies and Chapter meetings in secret and at night.
9. That the Templars abused the duties of charity and hospitality and used illegal means to acquire property and increase their wealth.

For an exhaustive study of the trial, see Malcolm Barber, *The Trial of the Templars* (Cambridge University Press, 1978). Edward Burman's *Supremely Abominable Crimes* (Allison & Busby, 1994) focuses on the Paris hearings of 1310. For other aspects of the trial, see the work of Jochen Burgtorf, Paul F. Crawford, Helen J. Nicholson and Anne Gilmour-Bryson.

Bibliography

Orthodox

Malcolm Barber, *The Trial of the Templars* (Cambridge University Press, 1978; second edition 2006); *The New Knighthood: A History of the Order of the Temple* (Cambridge University Press, 1994)

Malcolm Barber and Keith Bate (translators and editors), *The Templars: Selected Sources* (Manchester Medieval Sources Series, Manchester University Press, 2002)

Jochen Burgtorf, Paul F. Crawford and Helen J. Nicholson (editors), *The Debate on the Trial of the Templars (1307–1314)* (Ashgate Publishing, 2010)

Edward Burman, *Supremely Abominable Crimes: The Trial of the Knights Templar* (Allison & Busby, 1994); *The Templars: Knights of God* (Inner Traditions, 1990)

Michael J Carroll, *The Knights Templar and Ireland* (Bantry Studio Publications, 2006)

Alain Demurger, *The Last Templar: The Tragedy of Jacques de Molay, Last Grand Master of the Temple* (Profile Books, 2004)

Robert Ferguson, *The Knights Templar and Scotland* (The History Press, 2010)

Barbara Frale, *The Templars: The Secret History Revealed* (Maverick House, 2009); *The Templars and the Shroud of Christ* (Maverick House, 2011)

Anne Gilmour-Bryson, *The Trial of the Templars in the Papal State and the Abruzzi* (Biblioteca apostolica Vaticana, 1982); *The Trial of the Templars in Cyprus: A Complete English Edition* (Brill, 1998)

Michael Haag, *The Tragedy of the Templars: The Rise and Fall of the Crusader States* (Profile Books, 2012)

Stephen Howarth, *The Knights Templar: The Essential History* (Continuum Books, 2006)

Evelyn Lord, *The Knights Templar in Britain* (Longman, 2004); *The Templar's Curse* (Pearson, 2008)

Gordon Napier, *The Rise and Fall of the Knights Templar: The Order of the Temple, 1118–1314 – A True History of Faith, Glory, Betrayal and Tragedy* (The History Press, 2007)

Helen Nicholson, *Templars, Hospitallers and Teutonic Knights: Images of the Military Orders* (Leicester University Press, 1993); *Love, War and the Grail: Templars, Hospitallers and Teutonic Knights in Medieval Epic and Romance, 1150–1500* (Brill, 2000); *The Knights Templar on Trial: The Trial of the Templars in the British Isles, 1308–11* (The History Press, 2009); *A Brief History of the Knights Templar* (Constable and Robinson, 2010; revised, non-illustrated edition of the author's earlier *The Knights Templar: A New History* – see *Illustrated*, below)

Karen Ralls, *Knights Templar Encyclopaedia* (New Page Books, 2007)

Piers Paul Read, *The Templars* (Weidenfeld & Nicholson, 1999)

Jochen Schenk, *Templar Families: Landowning Families and the Order of the Temple in France, c.1120–1307* (Cambridge University Press, 2012)

Dominic Selwood, *Knights of the Cloister: Templars and Hospitallers in Central-Southern Occitania, c.1100–c.1300* (Boydell Press, 1999)

Desmond Seward, *The Monks of War: The Military Religious Orders* (Penguin Books, 1992)

Judi Upton-Ward (trans.), *The Rule of the Templars: The French Text of the Rule of the Order of Knights Templar* (Boydell Press, 1992)

History and Myth

Juliet Faith, *Glastonbury, The Templars and The Sovran Cloth: A New Perspective on the Grail Legends* (The History Press, 2012)

Michael Haag, *The Templars: History & Myth* (Profile Books, 2008)

Christopher Hodapp and Alice Von Kannon, *The Templar Code for Dummies* (Wiley Publishing, 2007)

Gordon Napier, *A–Z of the Knights Templar: A Guide to their History and Legacy* (The History Press, 2008)

Peter Partner, *The Murdered Magicians* (Oxford University Press, 1981); republished as *The Knights Templar and their Myth* (Inner Traditions, 1990)

Karen Ralls, *The Templars and the Grail* (Quest Books, 2003)

Illustrated

Simon Brighton, *In Search of the Knights Templar: A Guide to the Sites in Britain* (Weidenfeld & Nicholson, 2006)

Stephen Dafoe, *Nobly Born: An Illustrated History of the Knights Templar* (Lewis Masonic, 2007)

Juliet Faith, *The Knights Templar in Somerset* (The History Press, 2009)

Susie Hodge, *The Secret History of the Knights Templar* (US: *The Knights Templar: Discovering the Myth and Reality of a Legendary Brotherhood*) (Lorenz Books 2006; US: Hermes House); *Secrets of the Knights Templar: The Hidden History of the World's Most Powerful Order* (as S J Hodge; Quercus, 2013)

Diane Holloway and Trish Colton, *The Knights Templar in Yorkshire* (The History Press, 2008)

Helen Nicholson, *The Knights Templar: A New History* (Sutton, 2001)

Helen Nicholson and Wayne Reynolds, *Knight Templar 1120–1312* (Osprey, 2004)

Speculative

Juan Garcia Atienza, *The Knights Templar in the Golden Age of Spain: Their Hidden History on the Iberian Peninsula* (Destiny Books, 2006)

Michael Baigent, Richard Leigh and Henry Lincoln, *The Holy Blood and the Holy Grail* (Jonathan Cape, 1982)

Michael Baigent and Richard Leigh, *The Temple and the Lodge* (Jonathan Cape, 1989)

Françine Bernier, *The Templars' Legacy in Montreal, the New Jerusalem* (Frontier Sciences Foundation, 2002)

Alan Butler and Stephen Dafoe, *The Warriors and the Bankers* (Templar Books, 1998); *The Templar Continuum* (Templar Books, 1999); *The Knights Templar Revealed: The Secrets of the Cistercian Legacy* (Robinson Publishing, 2006)

EC Coleman, *The Grail Chronicles: Tracing the Holy Grail from the Last Supper to its Current Location* (The History Press, 2010)

Stephen Dafoe, *The Compasses and the Cross: A History of the Masonic Knights Templar* (Ian Allan, 2008)

Erling Haagensen and Henry Lincoln, *The Templars' Secret Island* (Weidenfeld & Nicholson, 2002)

Christopher Knight and Robert Lomas, *The Second Messiah* (Random

House, 1997)

Keith Laidler, *The Head of God: The Lost Treasure of the Templars* (Weidenfeld & Nicholson, 1998); *The Divine Deception* (Headline, 2000)

Ruggero Marino, *Christopher Columbus, the Last Templar* (Destiny Books, 2007)

Jean Markale, *The Templar Treasure at Gisors* (Inner Traditions, 2003)

Gil McHattie (editor), *The Knights Templar: Influences from the Past and Impulses for the Future* (Temple Lodge Publishing, 2011)

Graham Phillips, *The Templars and the Ark of the Covenant* (Bear and Company, 2004)

Lynne Picknett and Clive Prince, *The Templar Revelation* (Bantam, 1997; revised edition, 2007)

Andrew Sinclair, *The Sword and the Grail* (Century, 1993); *The Secret Scroll* (Sinclair Stevenson, 2001)

Steven Sora, *Lost Treasure of the Knights Templar: Solving the Oak Island Mystery* (Destiny Books, 1999)

Tim Wallace-Murphy and Marilyn Hopkins, *Rosslyn: Guardian of the Secrets of the Holy Grail* (Element, 1999); *Templars in America: From the Crusades to the New World* (Red Wheel/Weiser, 2004)

Tim Wallace-Murphy, *The Knights of the Holy Grail: The Secret History of the Knights Templar* (Watkins Publishing, 2007)

Related Interest

Karen Armstrong, *A Short History of Myth* (Canongate, 2005)

Richard Barber, *The Holy Grail: The History of a Legend* (Penguin, 2005)

WB Bartlett, *The Assassins: The Story of Islam's Medieval Secret Sect* (Sutton, 2001)

Jonathan Black, *The Secret History of the World* (Quercus, 2007); *The Sacred History* (Quercus, 2013)

Nigel Bryant (trans.), *The High Book of the Grail: A Translation of the Thirteenth-Century Romance of 'Perlesvaus'* (DS Brewer, 1978)

Chrétien de Troyes, Nigel Bryant (trans.), *Perceval: The Story of the Grail* (DS Brewer, 1986)

Edward Burman, *The Assassins* (Crucible, 1987)

E Christiansen, *The Northern Crusades: The Baltic and the Catholic Frontier 1100–1525* (Macmillan, 1980)

Lindsay Clarke, *Parzival and the Stone from Heaven* (Godstow Press, 2011)

BIBLIOGRAPHY

Malcolm Godwin, *The Holy Grail* (Bloomsbury, 1994)

William J Hamblin and David Rolph Seely, *Solomon's Temple: Myth and History* (Thames and Hudson, 2007)

Nick Harding, *Secret Societies* (Pocket Essentials, 2005)

Joinville and Villehardouin, *Chronicles of the Crusades* (Penguin Classics, 1963)

David Marcombe, *Leper Knights: The Order of St Lazarus of Jerusalem in England, c.1150–1544* (Boydell Press, 2003)

Helen Nicholson, *The Knights Hospitaller* (Boydell Press, 2001)

Mike Paine, *The Crusades* (Pocket Essentials, 2005)

Jonathan Riley-Smith, *The Knights of St John in Jerusalem and Cyprus 1050–1310* (Macmillan, 1967); *The Oxford Illustrated History of the Crusades* (as editor, Oxford University Press, 1995)

Robert de Boron, Nigel Bryant (trans.), *Merlin and the Grail: Joseph of Arimathea, Merlin, Perceval – The Trilogy of Arthurian Prose Romances Attributed to Robert de Boron* (DS Brewer, 2005)

Sir Steven Runciman, *A History of the Crusades* (3 Vols) (Penguin Books 1990–91)

Idries Shah, *The Sufis* (Octagon, 1964)

RC Smail, *Crusading Warfare, 1097–1193* (Cambridge University Press, 1995)

Yuri Stoyanov, *The Other God: Dualist Religion from Antiquity to the Cathar Heresy* (Yale University Press, 2000)

Christopher Tyerman, *God's War: A New History of the Crusades* (Allen Lane, 2006)

Tim Wallace-Murphy, *What Islam Did for Us: Understanding Islam's Contribution to Western Civilization* (Watkins Publishing, 2006)

Ian Wilson, *The Turin Shroud: The Burial Cloth of Jesus?* (Transworld, 1979); *Secret Places, Holy Faces* (Transworld, 1991)

William Urban, *The Teutonic Knights: A Military History* (Greenhill Books, 2003)

Wolfram von Eschenbach, *Parzival* (trans. AT Hatto, Penguin Books, 1980); *Parzival with Titurel and the Love Lyrics* (trans. Cyril Edwards, Boydell Press, 2004)

Theodore Ziolkowski, *Lure of the Arcane: The Literature of Cult and Conspiracy* (Johns Hopkins University Press, 2013)

The Templars in Fiction

* denotes first in a series

Maureen Ash, *The Alehouse Murders* (Berkley, 2007)*
Steve Berry, *The Templar Legacy* (Bantam, 2005)*
Dan Brown, *The Da Vinci Code* (Bantam, 2003)
Paul Christopher, *The Sword of the Templars* (Penguin Books, 2011)*
Stephen Dafoe and Bob Prodor, *Outremer: The Saga of the Knights Templar* (Templar Comics, 2008)
John Paul Davis, *The Templar Agenda* (John Paul Davis, 2011)
Paul Doherty, *The Templar* (Headline, 2007)*
Lawrence Durrell, *Constance* (Penguin, 1984)
Umberto Eco, *Foucault's Pendulum* (Secker & Warburg, 1989)
Jan Guillou, *The Road to Jerusalem* (HarperCollins, 2009)*
MR James, '"Oh, Whistle, and I'll Come to You, My Lad"' in *Count Magnus and Other Ghost Stories* (Penguin, 2006)
Michael Jecks, *The Last Templar* (Headline, 1994)*
Raymound Khoury, *The Last Templar* (Orion, 2006)*
Katherine Kurtz and Deborah Turner Harris, *The Temple and the Stone** (Warner Books, 1999)
Julia Navarro, *The Brotherhood of the Holy Shroud* (John Murray, 2008)
CM Palov, *The Templar's Code* (Penguin Books, 2010)
Mario Reading, *The Templar Prophecy* (Corvus, 2014)
Phil Rickman, *The Fabric of Sin* (Quercus, 2007)
Walter Scott, *Ivanhoe* (Penguin Classics, 2003); *The Talisman* (Dodo Press, 2005)
Dominic Selwood, *The Sword of Moses* (Corax, 2013)
William Watson, *The Last of the Templars* (Harvill, 1979)
Jack Whyte, *Knights of the Black and White* (Penguin Books, 2006)*
Robyn Young, *Brethren* (Hodder & Stoughton, 2006)*

Internet

www.templarhistory.com

Index

INDEX